Thin thighs in thirty years

Other Cathy books from Andrews, McMeel & Parker

Wake me up when I'm a size 5

Men should come with instruction booklets

A mouthful of breath mints and no one to kiss

Another Saturday night of wild and reckless abandon

How to get rich, fall in love, lose weight, and solve all your problems
   by saying "no"

Eat your way to a better relationship

Thin thighs in thirty years

A cathy Collection

by Cathy Guisewite

Andrews, McMeel & Parker
A Universal Press Syndicate Affiliate
Kansas City • New York

ISBN: 0-8362-2081-1

Library of Congress Catalog Card Number: 86-71301

3

Panel 1: HOLD ALL MY CALLS, CHARLENE. I HAVE TO GET SOME WORK DONE TODAY. / WHAT IF MAX CALLS?

Panel 2: EXCEPT MAX. I'LL TALK TO MAX. I'LL TALK TO IRVING. / IRVING? ANDREA?

Panel 3: I'LL TALK TO ANDREA, IRVING, MAX, MY PARENTS, ALL FRIENDS, AND ANYONE OFFERING ME PRIZE MONEY.

Panel 4: HOLD ONLY THOSE CALLS THAT HAVE ANYTHING TO DO WITH MY JOB.

Panel 5: IT'S 7:00, CATHY. AREN'T YOU LEAVING? / NO. I'M WAITING FOR EVERYONE ELSE TO LEAVE SO I CAN GET SOME WORK DONE. AREN'T YOU LEAVING??

Panel 6: NO. I'M WAITING FOR EVERYONE TO LEAVE SO I CAN GET SOME WORK DONE. / I'M WAITING FOR EVERYONE TO LEAVE SO I CAN GET SOME WORK DONE!!

Panel 7: ON THE COUNT OF THREE, WE ARE ALL LEAVING. ONE.. ..TWO...THREE.....LEAVE!

Panel 8: I'M GOING TO BE LATER THAN I THOUGHT, MAX. I CAN'T SEEM TO LOSE THE TEAM SPIRIT.

Panel 9: ATTENTION ALL EMPLOYEES, AND WELCOME TO THE CORPORATE SOFTBALL SEASON.

Panel 10: JEFF, WHO HASN'T SCORED SINCE 1983 AND IS 0-FOR-16 THIS YEAR, IS GIVING HIS BEST PITCH TO LYNN, WHO SWINGS AND JUST MISSES HIS NOSE... ...MEANWHILE, TOM AND MARY ARE WARMING EACH OTHER UP...

Panel 11: ...WHILE JOE HAS ONCE AGAIN STRUCK OUT WITH CINDY, AND IN A BRILLIANT DOUBLE PLAY, KAREN SEEMS TO BE HEADING FOR HOME WITH BOTH TED AND BILL....

Panel 12: YOU'RE SUPPOSED TO BE TALKING ABOUT THE PEOPLE WHO ARE PLAYING SOFTBALL, CHARLENE. / WHAT FOR?

BING! IT'S TIME, CATHY. YEAH, JUST A SEC...

IT'S TIME TO MARRY. WHAT??
TIME TO WED. WED? WHAT?!
TIME TO JOIN A MAN AND MOVE FORWARD. WHAT?? WHAT??

ANDREA, YOU HAVEN'T EVEN SPOKEN TO A MAN IN TEN YEARS! WHAT HAPPENED IN THE LAST SIX MINUTES THAT MADE YOU WANT TO MARRY ONE?!!

I DON'T KNOW. SOMETHING CHANGED INSIDE. YOU WERE STANDING TOO CLOSE TO THE MICROWAVE!!

IT JUST SEEMS LIKE IT'S TIME TO GET MARRIED AND INTO THE NEXT PHASE OF LIFE, CATHY. ANDREA, EVER SINCE I'VE KNOWN YOU, YOU'VE RIDICULED MY DREAMS OF MARRIAGE.

YOU'VE INSULTED MY BOYFRIENDS, ALIENATED MY DATES AND MADE MY LIFE A TOTAL MISERY OF INTROSPECTION!....YOU CANNOT GET MARRIED!

WHY NOT?

WHO WILL I HAVE FUN WITH??

JULY 8: BUY WEDDING DRESS
JULY 15: CHOOSE CATERER
JULY 22: SIGN PRE-NUPTIALS
JULY 29: SEND INVITATIONS

IT WILL BE TIGHT, BUT I THINK I CAN STILL MAKE IT FOR AN AUGUST WEDDING, CATHY.

AREN'T YOU LEAVING SOMETHING OUT, ANDREA?

JULY 1-7: MEET HUSBAND.

9

YOU HAVEN'T BEEN ON A DATE IN TEN YEARS. YOU'RE NOT GOING TO JUST WALTZ INTO A SUSHI BAR AND MEET SOMEONE.

WHY NOT, CATHY?

ANDREA, THE SUBTLETIES OF MODERN FLIRTATION ARE AN ART FORM TO BE STUDIED... THE GLANCES...THE BLINKS... THE POUTS...THE NODS...

I HAVEN'T BEEN WITH A MAN IN TEN YEARS. ANY TAKERS?

JUST TESTING.

BLINK BLINK

POUT

NOD

BLINK

SO ARE YOU INTERESTED, OR WHAT?

I'VE ONLY KNOWN YOU FOR 13 SECONDS.

I DON'T HAVE TIME TO SPEND A YEAR IN A RELATIONSHIP SEEING WHETHER OR NOT IT WILL GO ANYWHERE...I DON'T EVEN HAVE A MONTH TO SPEND.

FRANKLY, IF THIS RELATIONSHIP DOESN'T PROMISE TO DELIVER WITHIN 24 HOURS, I'LL LOOK FOR ANOTHER ONE THAT WILL!

WE'RE IN THE FEDERAL EXPRESS YEARS OF OUR LOVE LIVES.

I'M SO TIRED OF HEARING WOMEN COMPLAIN ABOUT THE LACK OF MEN IN THEIR LIVES WHEN THEY DO NOTHING TO CHANGE IT, CATHY.

DO WE GO TO THE STORE AND WAIT FOR FOOD TO JUMP IN OUR BASKETS?...NO! DO WE SECRETLY HOPE A BOX OF LASAGNA WILL INVITE ITSELF OVER??...NO!

WHEN A PERSON WANTS SOMETHING, SHE HAS TO TAKE ACTIONS TO GET IT!!

I'M ON TO YOU NOW, POT ROAST!!

BUTCHER DEPT

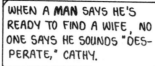

Panel 1:
ANDREA, YOU CAN'T WALK AROUND ANNOUNCING THAT YOU'RE LOOKING FOR A HUSBAND. YOU SOUND DESPERATE.
DON'T BE RIDICULOUS.

Panel 2:
WHEN A MAN SAYS HE'S READY TO FIND A WIFE, NO ONE SAYS HE SOUNDS "DESPERATE," CATHY.

Panel 3:
MEN WHO ARE MATURE ENOUGH TO EXPRESS A DESIRE FOR A SERIOUS, COMMITTED RELATIONSHIP ARE CALLED SOMETHING ENTIRELY DIFFERENT !!

Panel 4:
"INVISIBLE".
HI. I'M LOOKING FOR A HUSBAND.
OOPS. GOTTA GO.

Panel 5:
WE USED TO SIT HERE AFTER WORK AND JUDGE PEOPLE STRICTLY ON THEIR LOOKS.

Panel 6:
NOW WE JUDGE EACH OTHER ON MORE SUBTLE QUALITIES.

Panel 7:
"IS HE GOOD FOR ME?" "DOES HE OFFER SOMETHING I'M LACKING?" "WOULD HE HELP MY LIFE BE BETTER BALANCED?"

Panel 8:
IT USED TO BE A MEAT MARKET. NOW IT'S A VEGETABLE MARKET.

Panel 9:
THESE ARE THE QUALITIES I'D LIKE TO FIND IN A MAN... THESE ARE THE QUALITIES I'M WILLING TO PUT UP WITH....

Panel 10:
AND THESE ARE THE QUALITIES I FIND UTTERLY REPULSIVE AND THAT I WOULD NOT TOLERATE UNDER ANY CONDITION.

Panel 11:
YO, SWEETHEART! LOVE THE MUSCLE TONE! LET'S GET CRAZY AT MY CONDO!

Panel 12:
LIKE A BUG TO FLYPAPER.

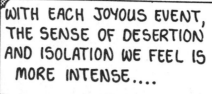
WE LAUGH ABOUT ALL OUR FRIENDS GETTING MARRIED, BUT WHEN IT HAPPENS, IT ISN'T THAT FUNNY.

WITH EACH JOYOUS EVENT, THE SENSE OF DESERTION AND ISOLATION WE FEEL IS MORE INTENSE....

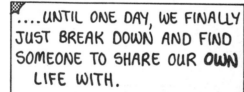
....UNTIL ONE DAY, WE FINALLY JUST BREAK DOWN AND FIND SOMEONE TO SHARE OUR **OWN** LIFE WITH.

SARA LEE: THE ONE WOMAN WHO WILL NEVER ABANDON ME.

FIRST I THOUGHT I'D GET MARRIED IN THE TRADITIONAL INDIAN GAUZE CAPE WITH A HAIKU AND LUTE MUSIC CEREMONY, CATHY.

...THEN I THOUGHT, NO. I'LL BE DIFFERENT. I'LL MARRY IN A 3-PIECE SUIT!...THEN I THOUGHT, NO. WHY NOT REALLY MAKE MY OWN STATEMENT?!

...MAYBE IN SOMETHING WHITE ...A LONG WHITE LACE AND SATIN GOWN WITH A VEIL, AND MAYBE...YES!.. MAYBE TUXEDOS FOR THE MEN!!!

ANOTHER REBEL HITS THE BRIDAL SALON.

I CAN SHOW YOU DRESSES IN NOVEMBER... THEN IT WILL BE 4 MONTHS TO ORDER....2 MONTHS TO ALTER...3 MONTHS TO RE-ORDER... 1 MONTH TO...

IT TAKES A YEAR TO GET A WEDDING DRESS?? HOW DO WOMEN STAND FOR THIS?!

OH, THE YOUNG ONES USED TO GET IMPATIENT, BUT MANY OF OUR BRIDES ARE OLDER THESE DAYS.

I CAN SEE WHY.

HELLO...DID MY GOWN COME IN YET?

"ONE YEAR BEFORE WEDDING: RESERVE RECEPTION HALL."

"ONE YEAR". GET REAL.

"SIX MONTHS BEFORE WEDDING: ENGRAVE INVITATIONS, ORDER CAKE, HIRE BAND..."

THAT'S RIDICULOUS.

THIS ARCHAIC TIMETABLE HAS NOTHING TO DO WITH THE FAST-PACED LIFE OF THE CONTEMPORARY BUSINESSWOMAN!!

WHY NOT?

NONE OF US HAS EVER HAD A RELATIONSHIP THAT LASTED THAT LONG.

WHEN THERE'S JUST ONE OF YOU, YOU CAN EAT EVERY MEAL WITH ONE LITTLE MUG AND A ROLL OF PAPER TOWELS.

GIFT REGISTRY

WHEN THERE ARE GOING TO BE TWO OF YOU, SUDDENLY YOU'RE SIGNING UP FOR GIANT TUREENS, POTS, PLATTERS AND GRAVY BOATS.

IT'S THE START OF A WHOLE NEW WAY OF LIFE, CATHY.

OBESITY.

GIFT REGISTRY

A MAN LOOKING FOR A WIFE IS "SINCERE". A WOMAN LOOKING FOR A HUSBAND IS "DESPERATE."

A MAN LOOKING FOR A WIFE IS "MATURE". A WOMAN LOOKING FOR A HUSBAND IS "DESPERATE".

A MAN LOOKING FOR A WIFE IS "CARING," "OPEN," AND "ADULT." A WOMAN LOOKING FOR A HUSBAND IS "DESPERATE, DESPERATE, DESPERATE"!

MAKES YOU FEEL KIND OF DESPERATE, DOESN'T IT?

..MBLGPF..

WHEN YOU MEET A MAN, YOU NEED TO SENSE WHAT HE LIKES AND TRANSFORM YOURSELF ACCORDINGLY.

CATHY, THAT'S WHAT YOU DID WITH IRVING, GRANT, JAKE, PAUL, DAVID, TED, AND MARK AND IT FAILED.

FOR TEN YEARS YOU'VE USED THE EXACT SAME APPROACH, AND FOR TEN YEARS IT'S FAILED THE EXACT SAME WAY. WHY NOT TRY MY METHOD??

WHAT IF IT DOESN'T WORK?

GOOD LOOKS JUST DON'T DO IT FOR ME ANYMORE, CATHY.

I KNOW. I WANT A MAN OF INTELLIGENCE AND DEPTH.

TICKETS

AND SAVVY. HE MUST HAVE FINANCIAL SAVVY.

AND COMPUTER LITERACY.

POLITICAL ASTUTENESS!

REFINEMENT! ELEGANCE!

SILVERADO
NOW PLAYING

I WANT A COWBOY.

ONE PIE. TWO FORKS.

After theatre specials:

HI. I JUST SAW YOU COMING OUT OF "SILVERADO." MIND IF I JOIN YOU?

YES. A THIRD PERSON WOULD BE A REAL INTRUSION TONIGHT.

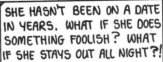

THE MOVIE MADE US WANT TO JUST SIT AND REVEL IN THE SPECIAL BONDS THAT OUR OWN FRIENDSHIP WAS BUILT ON.

TWO PIES. ONE FORK.

After theatre specials:

IT'S ALMOST MIDNIGHT AND ANDREA ISN'T HOME YET, MAX!

SO WHAT?

SHE HASN'T BEEN ON A DATE IN YEARS. WHAT IF SHE DOES SOMETHING FOOLISH? WHAT IF SHE STAYS OUT ALL NIGHT?!

CATHY, WHAT'S WRONG WITH A GROWN WOMAN STAYING OUT ALL NIGHT?

I DON'T WANT TO HAVE TO WAIT UNTIL MORNING TO FIND OUT WHAT WENT ON!!!

18

Panel 1: YOU KNOW WHAT'S WRONG WITH MEN? YOU'RE PICKY.

Panel 2: IF A WOMAN ISN'T 100% PERFECT, YOU DON'T EVEN GIVE HER A CHANCE. YOU'RE PICKY, PICKY, PICKY!!

Panel 3: HAH! / BLEAH!

Panel 4: WHAT'S WRONG? / I COULD NEVER DATE A MAN WITH GOLD FILLINGS.

Panel 5: IN A FINAL ATTEMPT TO MEET A HUSBAND, ANDREA IS PLANTING HERSELF IN FRONT OF THE RADICCHIO LETTUCE IN THE GOURMET GROCERY EVERY NIGHT THIS WEEK.

Panel 6: THE GROCERY STORE?? / YEAH...

Panel 7: AFTER ALL THE PHONY PLACES SINGLES HAVE TRIED, THE GROCERY STORE HAS EMERGED AS THE ONE FINAL ENVIRONMENT OFFERING AN ATMOSPHERE OF CASUALNESS AND SPONTANEITY.

Panel 8: MOVE OVER, GIRLS. I SAW HIM FIRST! / le Produce

Panel 9: I HAVE ANOTHER CALL, IRVING. JUST A SEC, OKAY? / CATHY, I'VE BEEN TRYING TO TALK TO YOU ALL WEEK!

Panel 10: ...I'M ON ANOTHER CALL, MOM. CAN YOU WAIT A MINUTE? / I'M YOUR MOTHER. I'M USED TO COMING LAST.

Panel 11: ...IRVING, I REALLY HAVE TO TAKE THE OTHER CALL... / SURE. LET ME KNOW WHEN I MOVE FROM "CALL BACK LATER" STATUS TO "TALK TO NOW" STATUS!

Panel 12: THE REST OF THE WORLD GOT "CALL WAITING." I GOT "GUILT WAITING."

20

21

REGARDING MY MEMO...

I DO NOT HAVE TIME FOR YOUR PICKY MEMOS TODAY, MR. PINKLEY.

MORRIE NEEDS 2 SECONDS. LINE 3.

PICKY MEMOS... 2-SECOND CALLS... IDIOTIC MEETINGS... WHEN AM I SUPPOSED TO GET THE REAL WORK DONE ??!

CAN YOU LOOK AT THIS FOR A MINUTE, CATHY?

THIS WILL JUST TAKE A SECOND...

5 MINUTES AND YOU'RE OUT OF HERE.

I'M BATTLING MONSTERS AND LOSING TO BUGS.

I'LL BARBECUE THE STEAKS, CATHY. YOU MAKE THE POTATO SALAD, FRUIT SALAD, CORN, COLE SLAW, ROLLS, DIPS, DRINKS AND DESSERT!

WHY DON'T I BARBECUE THE STEAKS AND YOU DO ALL THE OTHER STUFF?

NAH... I WOULDN'T WANT YOU TO GET ALL DIRTY.

HE JUST SAID, "HELLO", CATHY. WHY WERE YOU SO WEIRD??

THE FATTER I GET, THE MORE MY PERSONALITY DISAPPEARS, CHARLENE.

TODAY IT SEEMS TO HAVE VANISHED COMPLETELY.

MUTINY ON THE BOUNTIFUL.

22

Panel 1:
I'VE HAD THREE DIALOGUES, NO DATES, CATHY.

MAYBE THIS ISN'T THE BEST PLACE TO MEET SOMEONE, ANDREA.

le Produce

Panel 2:
NO, IT'S PERFECT. ANY MAN WITH THE BRAINS TO BE SHOPPING FOR ENDIVE AND FRESH BASIL IS GOING TO HAVE AN ENLIGHTENED ATTITUDE ABOUT HIS RELATIONSHIPS.

Panel 3:
HI. DO YOU KNOW HOW TO...

YOU PIG! WHY DO YOU ASSUME I CAN COOK JUST BECAUSE I'M A WOMAN?!

Panel 4:
FOUR DIALOGUES, NO DATES.

le Produce

Panel 5:
MY DIVORCE IS FINAL AND I'M READY TO PARTY!

SINGLE FOR 15 MINUTES. NO GOOD.

Panel 6:
THIS IS THE KIND JANET AND I USED TO HAVE!

SINGLE FOR 6 MONTHS. NO GOOD.

Panel 7:
EVERY NIGHT I HAVE A GLASS OF WINE BEFORE I CALL MY MOTHER.

SINGLE FOR 35 YEARS. NO GOOD.

Panel 8:
EVERYONE WAS THE RIGHT AGE, BUT NO ONE WAS THE RIGHT VINTAGE.

le Produce

Panel 9:
THE TRADITIONAL WEDDING HAS 150 GUESTS AND FIVE BRIDESMAIDS, CATHY.

YOU'RE NOT GOING TO DO THAT ARE YOU, ANDREA?

Panel 10:
CERTAINLY NOT. FOR TEN YEARS MY LIFE HAS BEEN SUPPORTED AND NURTURED BY MY NETWORK OF SINGLE WOMEN FRIENDS.

Panel 11:
I OWE IT TO ALL OF US TO HAVE A CEREMONY THAT REFLECTS WHAT WE'VE ALL BEEN THROUGH TOGETHER!!

Panel 12:
WHAT ARE YOU GOING TO HAVE?

150 BRIDESMAIDS AND FIVE GUESTS.

HALFWAY THROUGH BRIDE'S MAGAZINE ANDREA QUIT LAUGHING AT THE TUXEDOS.

UH OH.

"MS. HOSTILITY 1985" IS PLANNING A BIG, TRADITIONAL WEDDING NOW?

YEAH... HOW COULD A BRIGHT WOMAN LIKE HER LOOK THROUGH THESE PAGES AND....

WAAAHH !!

IT MUST BE SOMETHING IN THE INK.

ANDREA, YOU'VE BEEN THROUGH THE CARRYOUT LINE 8 TIMES. CAN'T WE GO?

NOT YET. A GUY WITH PORSCHE KEYS JUST GOT IN LINE.

WELL?

HE'S MARRIED. BUT A MAN CARRYING A LEGAL PAD JUST WALKED IN.

WELL?

GAY. BUT SOMEONE IN SURGICAL SCRUBS JUST CAME IN.

THIS ISN'T DINNER. IT'S A DOWRY.

THE ONLY REASON PEOPLE DON'T FIND SOMEONE TO MARRY IS THAT THEY KEEP CHANGING THEIR MINDS ABOUT WHAT THEY WANT.

IMAGINE IF YOU SHOPPED FOR SHAMPOO IN THAT KIND OF CONFUSED STUPOR, CATHY...

YOU'D HAVE A CABINET FULL OF SHAMPOO, AND YOU'D STILL BE OUT LOOKING FOR SHAMPOO EVERY WEEK !!

WHY DO YOU SAY "YOU'D"?

WITH THIS INFORMATION ACCESS SYSTEM I CAN TALK TO PEOPLE ALL OVER THE COUNTRY ON MY COMPUTER SCREEN... AND SUDDENLY, THERE HE WAS!!

"HE"?

HE. MR. RIGHT. MR. WONDERFUL. WE TALKED ALL NIGHT!

YOU TALKED ALL NIGHT?

IT'S THE '80s DREAM COME TRUE, CATHY.

YOU MET A MAN WITHOUT HAVING TO PUT ON A LEOTARD!!

WHAT DO YOU MEAN, HE'S PERFECT?? HE'S JUST A BUNCH OF WORDS ON YOUR MONITOR!

THAT'S THE BEAUTY OF ON-SCREEN DATING, CATHY.

YOU CAN'T JUDGE EACH OTHER ON LOOKS, DRESS, POSSESSIONS, ENVIRONMENT, HANDWRITING, CREDIT CARDS... ANYTHING.

FOR ONCE, ALL YOU HAVE IS AN HONEST EXCHANGE OF FEELINGS AND PHILOSOPHIES BETWEEN TWO INTELLIGENT PEOPLE.

YOU'RE BASING A RELATIONSHIP ON **THAT**??

TALK TO MY FIANCÉ ON THE MONITOR WHILE I GRAB SOME COFFEE, CATHY.

I DON'T KNOW ANYTHING ABOUT YOUR COMPUTER, ANDREA.

YOU DON'T HAVE TO. THIS IS JUST A SIMPLE INTERACTIVE VIDEOTEX SERVICE RUNNING THROUGH A 300 BAUD MODEM INTERFACED WITH A 256K PC. JUST REBOOT THE SYSTEM, STAY IN THE DEFAULT DRIVE, AND LOG ON WITH CONTROL/C AT THE ON-LINE MENU PROMPT!

YOU NEED TO KNOW ABSOLUTELY **NOTHING**!!

LAST DECADE WE LOST OUR INNOCENCE. THIS DECADE WE'VE LOST OUR IGNORANCE.

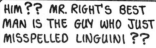
THIS IS HIM? THIS IS MR. RIGHT??

NO... THAT'S OUR BEST MAN.

HIM?? MR. RIGHT'S BEST MAN IS THE GUY WHO JUST MISSPELLED LINGUINI??

CATHY, WHEN YOU LOVE SOMEONE, YOU DON'T MAKE RASH JUDGMENTS ABOUT HIM BASED ON HIS FRIENDS.

HE WROTE, "I HOPE MY BUDDY'S LITTLE WOMAN CAN MAKE LINGUINI."

CANCEL THE ACCORDION PLAYER!!

ANDREA HAS MET THE MAN SHE WANTS TO MARRY AND MOM ISN'T HOME.

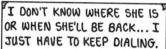

I DON'T KNOW WHERE SHE IS OR WHEN SHE'LL BE BACK... I JUST HAVE TO KEEP DIALING.

AT TIMES LIKE THIS WE NEED TO SAY THINGS TO OUR MOTHERS THAT WE COULD ONLY SAY TO A BEST FRIEND.

GET AN ANSWERING MACHINE!!!

THE MAN YOU PROPOSED TO ON YOUR COMPUTER IS ON HIS WAY OVER AND YOU'RE NOT NERVOUS TO SEE WHAT HE LOOKS LIKE??!

I'VE LOGGED 100 HOURS OF CONNECT TIME WITH HIM, CATHY.

I KNOW HE'S WISE, CARING, THOUGHTFUL, ENLIGHTENED AND COMPASSIONATE.

DING DONG

FOR ME TO JUDGE HIM ON PHYSICAL APPEARANCE WOULD MAKE A MOCKERY OF EVERYTHING I STAND FOR!

HE'S GORGEOUS.

THANK YOU, GOD.

29

ANDREA'S REALLY GOING TO GET MARRIED, MOM! MY LAST PILLAR OF SINGLE-NESS HAS CRUMBLED!!

THE FRIEND I'VE TRIED MOST TO EMU-LATE IS BE-COMING SOME-ONE'S WIFE!!

OH, CATHY, AT TIMES LIKE THIS A MOTHER HAS THOUGHTS SHE JUST CAN'T VERBALIZE.

YIPPEE.

WHAT DO YOU MEAN, I CAN'T GET ENGRAVED DOILIES BY NEXT WEEK?!

ANDREA, YOU'RE GETTING MAR-RIED IN A PASTA EMPORIUM TO A MAN YOU MET ON A COMPUTER SCREEN, WITH A MAID OF HONOR IN A SWEAT-SUIT AND YOUR MOTHER BEAMED IN VIA SATELLITE FROM A SELF-DEFENSE SEMI-NAR IN HAWAII.

WHY DO YOU CARE IF THERE ARE ENGRAVED DOILIES??!

I WANT EVERYTHING TO BE TRADITIONAL.

WHEN YOU'RE MARRIED, I WON'T BE ABLE TO CALL YOU IN THE MIDDLE OF THE NIGHT AND REHEARSE MY FIGHTS WITH IRVING.

PROBABLY NOT.

I WON'T BE ABLE TO LIE AROUND ON YOUR COUCH EVERY EVENING, WATCHING ALL YOUR MOVIE CHANNELS AND EATING ALL YOUR FOOD.

PROBABLY NOT.

I WON'T BE ABLE TO PLAN WHOLE WEEKENDS WITH YOU THAT I CANCEL AT THE LAST SECOND IF I GET A DATE.

PROBABLY NOT, CATHY.

HOW CAN YOU GIVE UP ALL THIS FREEDOM?!!

THE BASIC $300 PHOTO PACKAGE WILL BE FINE.

WHEN YOU'RE OLD AND DECREPIT, YOU'RE GOING TO WISH YOU'D POPPED FOR THE "MOONLIGHT MONTAGES."

SAMPL

WEDDING PHOTOS

WHEN YOUR CHILDREN ARE GROWN AND GONE, THE $40 EXTRA FOR "MISTY" LIGHTING IS GOING TO SEEM PRETTY INSIGNIFICANT.

WHEN IT'S JUST YOU AND HIM AND A BOOK OF FADED MEMORIES, YOU'RE GOING TO KICK YOURSELF FOR NOT GOING WITH THE 8x10'S!!

WHEN THEY SAY WEDDINGS ARE PLANNED FOR GRAND-PARENTS, I NEVER THOUGHT THEY'D MEAN US.

PHOTO STUDIO

BABIES BRIDES BAR MITZVAH

IF MY FIANCÉ CAN GO OUT ON THE TOWN FOR HIS BACHELOR PARTY, SO CAN WE!

YEAH! SO CAN WE!

WE'RE ADULTS! WHY NOT?!

WHY NOT?!

CONTEMPORARY WOMEN DO NOT SIT AT HOME WITH BAGS OVER OUR HEADS!!

MALE STRIPPERS TONIGHT

SHOW TIME

AACK! THIS IS SO SLEAZY!

GROSS! SLEAZY AND GROSS!

RAUNCHI-NESS TO THE MAX!!

Male Strippers Tonight

DISGUST-ING! DE-GRADING!

VILE DEGRAD-ING SLEAZE!

SLEAZY SLEAZY SLEAZY!

BLEAHHH!!

IS EVERYTHING OKAY HERE?

FINE, THANKS.

Male Strippers

THE MAID OF HONOR WILL WALK DOWN THE AISLE TO HERE...

WAAAHH!

PASTA EMPORIUM

...WHERE SHE'LL BE JOINED BY THE BRIDE AND...

WAAH!

YOU'RE MY BEST FRIEND, ANDREA! DON'T DO THIS! DON'T GROW UP! WAAAHH!!

IT'S TRADITIONAL FOR THE MAID OF HONOR TO GIVE A SHOWER.

IF THIS ISN'T GOING TO BE A WEIRD WEDDING, WHY IS THE MAID OF HONOR WEARING A SWEATSUIT?

MOM, THERE WILL BE NO PARA-CHUTES, NO GURUS, NO TRIB-AL DANCES, NO CHANTS....

...JUST A NICE NORMAL CEREMONY IN A PASTA EM-PORIUM WITH THE BRIDES-MAIDS IN SWEATSUITS AND MANY OF THE GUESTS ON COMPUTER SCREENS.

EVERY GENERATION FINDS A NEW WAY TO OFFEND THE RELATIVES.

AFTER TWO DECADES OF REJECTING MARRIAGE, RE-BELLING AGAINST MARRIAGE AND TOTALLY RESTRUCTUR-ING MARRIAGE, THE BABY BOOMERS ARE GETTING MARRIED.

TWENTY YEARS OF INTENSE INDIVIDUALISM LATER, THE CEREMONY MOST CHOSEN IS **NOT** SOME BIZARRE PERSON-AL DEMONSTRATION...

...BUT THE MOST BASIC RE-ENACTMENT OF THE SIMPLE HAPPY TRADITIONS WE GREW UP WITH...

.....AND ACTION!

WAAAH!

CUT!

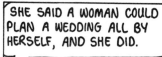

...IF ANYONE OBJECTS TO THIS WEDDING...

SMACK!

...SPEAK NOW OR FOREVER HOLD YOUR PEACE...

SMACK! SMACK!

...IF THERE ARE NO OBJECTIONS, THEN BY THE POWER VESTED IN ME, I NOW PRONOUNCE YOU HUSBAND AND WIFE.

MMFPH

AACK!

AACK!

YOU MAY NOW UNTANGLE THE BRIDE.

WASN'T IT A BEAUTIFUL WEDDING, IRVING, AND DIDN'T IT MAKE YOU THINK OF MARRIAGE YOURSELF ??

ANDREA AND

ISN'T IT ABOUT TIME FOR YOU TO BE TYING THE OLD KNOT ??

ANDREA AN

DIDN'T CATHY MAKE A BEAUTIFUL MAID OF HONOR? DON'T YOU WORRY THAT SOMEONE ELSE WILL SNATCH HER UP?

ANDREA AND

CATHY, WHY DON'T YOU GO STOP HER ??!

I HAVEN'T HEARD HIM GIVE ANY ANSWERS YET.

I SAW YOU LEAVE ANDREA'S WEDDING WITH IRVING, CATHY.

YES... YES, I DID.

I HOPE I DIDN'T EMBARRASS YOU BY GRILLING HIM ABOUT HIS OWN MARRIAGE PLANS.

OH, NO, MOM. DON'T BE SILLY.

IT DIDN'T BOTHER YOU WHEN I PUSHED YOU IN THE PATH OF THE BRIDAL BOUQUET AND SHRIEKED, "IRVING, SHE'S YOURS!" ??

OH, HA, HA! NO. NO PROBLEM!

DID YOU FIND OUT WHAT YOU WANTED?

YES. HE'S STILL AT HER PLACE.

CAN I PUT THIS HERE, CATHY?

NO! THAT'S THE DOOMED PILE.

NEW MAIL GOES IN THIS LITTLE PILE THAT I CAN STILL DEAL WITH... ONE-WEEK-OLD MAIL GOES IN THIS LITTLE PILE....

THE DOOMED PILE IS FOR THINGS THAT I'VE IGNORED, AVOIDED, RATIONALIZED AND HIDDEN FROM FOR SO LONG THAT I CAN'T EVEN LOOK AT THEM WITHOUT GETTING SICK.

IF YOU'RE NEVER GOING TO DO THAT STUFF, WHY DON'T YOU JUST THROW IT ALL AWAY?

IT WOULD SEEM SO UNPROFESSIONAL.

TOO SUMMERY.

TOO WINTERY.

TOO SUMMERY... TOO WINTERY... TOO SUMMERY... TOO WINTERY... TOO SUMMERY... TOO WINTERY...

WE'LL HOLD THE MEETING AS LONG AS WE CAN, CATHY. WHAT TIME CAN YOU BE IN?

9:00 A.M. DECEMBER 21.

I'M NOT JEALOUS THAT ANDREA FOUND A HUSBAND, JUST THAT SHE DOESN'T HAVE TO LOOK ANYMORE.

YEAH, I KNOW WHAT YOU MEAN, CHARLENE.

I ALWAYS FIGURED THAT BY THIS TIME IN OUR LIVES WE SHOULD BE ABLE TO QUIT TRYING SO HARD.

I DON'T KNOW HOW MANY MORE YEARS OF LOOKING THIS STUNNING I CAN TAKE, CATHY.

IT'S A QUESTION EVERY SINGLE WOMAN GRAPPLES WITH.

ARE WE DISAPPOINTED BECAUSE WE HAVEN'T FOUND TRUE LOVE OR BECAUSE WE HAVE TO KEEP SHAVING OUR LEGS EVERY DAY?

"SINGLE SERVING LASAGNA: MICROWAVE ON HIGH FOR 10 TO 15 MINUTES."

BING!

"LET STAND 3 MINUTES."

THEY DIDN'T SAY **WHERE** IT HAD TO STAND.

I'LL BE OVER IN HALF AN HOUR, IRVING.

I THOUGHT YOU WEREN'T GOING TO START SEEING IRVING ALL THE TIME AGAIN, CATHY.

YEAH, WELL...

EVEN IF YOU WERE GOING TO SEE HIM, YOU WEREN'T GOING TO GO TO HIS PLACE.

YEAH, WELL...

EVEN IF YOU WERE GOING TO GO TO HIS PLACE, YOU WEREN'T GOING TO ALTERNATE EQUALLY WITH HIM COMING TO YOUR PLACE.

I NEED A HUG FIRST. I'LL HAVE A REUNION WITH MY DIGNITY LATER.

PRODUCT TESTING LINE.

EGGS. AACK! SUMMER'S OVER AND I HAVEN'T HAD PEOPLE OVER FOR BRUNCH YET.

DAIRY   EGGS

MOPS. AACK! IT'S SEPTEMBER 24 AND I DIDN'T DO MY SPRING CLEANING YET!

VEGETABLES. AACK! I HAVEN'T BEEN TO THE HEALTH CLUB....FRUIT. AACK! I FORGOT TO CALL MOM!

MORE AND MORE BUSY COUPLES ARE OPTING FOR CARRY-OUT.

CASHIER

I MADE IT THROUGH MY BEST FRIEND'S WEDDING WITHOUT DESTROYING MY DIET.

I SURVIVED THE WEEK OF THE WEDDING... THE DAY OF THE WEDDING... THE NIGHT OF THE WEDDING.

ONE LITTLE PART OF ME IS PROUD. THE REST OF ME CAN'T STAND THE FACT THAT I MISSED SUCH A PERFECT EXCUSE TO EAT.

NOW THAT I'VE FINALLY LEARNED TO COPE WITH THE PRESENT, I'M PIGGING OUT IN RETROSPECT.

I'VE SPENT THE WHOLE DAY DEALING WITH THESE IDIOTIC SCRAPS OF PAPER, CHARLENE.

MEANINGLESS MEMOS... PICKY, INSIGNIFICANT PHONE CALLS...LUDICROUS NOTES...

NOW IRVING'S WAITING FOR ME AND I STILL HAVE TWO HOURS OF THESE MISERABLE MEDIOCRE DETAILS TO TAKE CARE OF.

WHY DON'T YOU JUST TELL HIM THAT?

I DON'T WANT MY WORK TO SOUND SO IMPORTANT.

...MY NOVEL? WHY, THANK YOU. THANK YOU. YES, I'M VERY EXCITED ABOUT THE MOVIE RIGHTS!

...ME FOR THE LEAD? OH, NO. DON'T BE SILLY...WELL...I SUPPOSE I COULD READ FOR .....OOPS! LOOK AT THE TIME.

... I'M SO SORRY TO CUT THIS SHORT, JOHNNY. ED... DOC...YOU'VE BEEN BEAUTIFUL...THANK YOU ALL......

WATCH OUT FOR PINKLEY TODAY. HE'S IN A TERRIBLE MOOD!

IT'S HARD TO RUIN A DAY THAT BEGAN BY BEING INTERVIEWED BY MY DEODORANT.

I DIDN'T HAVE TIME FOR LUNCH, CHARLENE. DO YOU HAVE ANY FOOD?

NO, BUT I THINK MORRIE HAS SOME CANDY IN HIS OFFICE.

DID MORRIE HAVE ANY LUCK?

NO, BUT HE SENT JILL TO ROOT THROUGH GRANT'S DESK FOR COOKIES AND SHAWN HAS A LEAD ON SOME OLD DONUTS!

THERE ARE REPORTS OF A BRAN MUFFIN IN ACCOUNTING AND IF WE FIND A LONG ENOUGH RULER, THERE'S ONE BAG OF AIRPLANE PEANUTS UNDER THE COPY MACHINE !!

IT'S AMAZING HOW EVERYONE PITCHES IN WHEN IT'S FOR A PROJECT WE ALL BELIEVE IN.

I LIKE BEING WITH HER. I DON'T HAVE TO IMPRESS HER.

I CAN BE SO RELAXED WITH HIM.

I CAN SAY ANYTHING I WANT.

I CAN WEAR ANYTHING I FEEL LIKE.

IT'S JUST LIKE BEING AT HOME!

FOR ONCE I CAN TOTALLY BE MYSELF!

HOO BOY, IS SHE LETTING HERSELF GO!

HOO BOY, IS HE LETTING HIMSELF GO!

IT USED TO BE IF YOU HADN'T HEARD THE SONG, YOU HADN'T HEARD THE SONG.

NOW IF YOU HAVEN'T HEARD THE SONG YOU ALSO HAVEN'T SEEN THE VIDEO, WATCHED THE REVIEWS, READ THE BOOK, GONE TO THE MOVIE, CAUGHT THE CLIPS, BOUGHT THE CONCEPT, WORN THE LOOK, DONE THE SOFTWARE OR DEVASTATED ANYONE WITH THE COLOGNE IT ALL INSPIRED.

WE'VE EVOLVED INTO A WHOLE NEW SPECIES.

IGNORAMUS MULTI-MEDIUS.

IF I QUIT SEEING IRVING, WOULD HE BE DEVASTATED?

WOULD HE TORMENT HIS NEXT GIRLFRIEND WITH STORIES OF ME?...WOULD HE TELL HIS CHILDREN ABOUT A WOMAN HE ONCE DATED?

FOR THE REST OF HIS LIFE, WOULD SOME LITTLE PART OF HIS MIND KEEP SNEAKING BACK TO ME, SECRETLY WONDERING, "WHAT IF....WHAT IF....."?

WHAT DID YOU SAY TO IRVING, CATHY?

NOTHING. I DON'T WANT TO BREAK UP WITH HIM UNTIL I'M SURE WE HAVE A FUTURE.

I AM **NOT** GOING ALL THE WAY TO THE STORE JUST BECAUSE THEY HAVE CHICKEN ON SALE, MOM.

HOW LONG COULD IT TAKE, CATHY?

...YOU JUST DRIVE TO THE STORE...GRAB THE CHICKEN AND HOLD THE PHONE...IS THAT DETERGENT FOR $1.29?!

...AND PAPER TOWELS FOR 59¢?!...WAIT..JUST LET ME GET SOME JUICE...DO YOU NEED BLEACH?...SESAME CRACKERS AND BAKING SODA WAIT...CHEESE HOT DOGS AND BROCCOLI..WAIT..WAIT...

YOU YOUNG PEOPLE HAVE NO CONCEPT OF SAVING MONEY.

MAY I HELP YOU?

YES. COULD YOU TELL ME WHY I'M THE ONE WHO FEELS LIKE THE WEIRDO IN HERE?

I'VE BEEN INTIMIDATED BY NEW FASHIONS FOR YEARS.

I'VE BEEN TOO SHY TO TRY THEM AND TOO INSECURE TO WEAR THEM.

BUT AFTER SEEING THIS YEAR'S STYLES, I'M FINALLY FEELING CONFIDENT ENOUGH TO MAKE MY OWN FASHION STATEMENT:

BLEAHH!!

I SPEND MY WHOLE LIFE AT THIS DESK. EVERY DAY MORE AND MORE PILES UP ON ME.

TO SOME, I'M BECOMING AN INTIMIDATING TOWER OF INFORMATION....

...BUT IF SOMEONE WOULD TAKE THE TIME, HE'D DISCOVER A TREASURE OF INCREDIBLE IDEAS AND OPINIONS BURIED JUST UNDER THE SURFACE.

SOME PEOPLE IDENTIFY WITH JANE FONDA. I IDENTIFY WITH AN "IN" BASKET.

ARE YOU OKAY, CATHY?

FINE, MOM. I'VE JUST HAD TO WORK LATE ALL WEEK.

I'VE HAD NO TIME TO CLEAN... NO TIME TO DO THE LAUNDRY... NO TIME TO WASH MY HAIR... NO TIME TO DO MY NAILS... NO TIME TO FIX MY FACE....

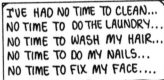

I'M GOING ON TWO HOURS OF SLEEP, SIX DAYS OF JUNK FOOD AND THE FINAL DREGS OF MY CLEAN CLOTHES.

DOESN'T IRVING MIND WHEN YOU WORK SO MUCH?

DON'T BE SILLY. MY CAREER IS MAKING ME MORE ATTRACTIVE TO HIM.

HAVE YOU MADE YOUR PLANS FOR CHRISTMAS YET, CATHY?

MOM, IT'S ONLY OCTOBER 12 AND YOU'VE BEEN ASKING ABOUT CHRISTMAS FOR A MONTH!

IT'S TOO EARLY TO THINK ABOUT CHRISTMAS! I DON'T WANT TO THINK ABOUT CHRISTMAS! ASK ME ABOUT ANYTHING, BUT DON'T ASK ME ABOUT CHRISTMAS!!

HAVE YOU MADE YOUR PLANS FOR THANKS- GIVING YET?

YES I'LL BE THERE FOR THANKSGIV- ING AND YES I'LL BRING A DATE. OKAY?? YES! YES!!

BINGO.

45

PLEASE TELL ME I RE-HEMMED THE SKIRT TO MY FALL SUIT OVER THE SUMMER.

PLEASE TELL ME I REPLACED THE BUTTONS.

PLEASE, PLEASE TELL ME I FOUND 15 MINUTES IN THE LAST 4 MONTHS TO STITCH UP THE SPLIT SEAMS AND FIX THE ZIPPER!

WE REAP WHAT WE DON'T SEW.

HERE YOU GO, CHARLENE! A FLUORESCENT SPANDEX MINI-SKIRT! HA, HA!

OH, PLEASE, CATHY! ARE THEY JOKING?!!

HA, HA! THIS IS SUPPOSED TO BE SEXY??!

HOO, HA! THIS IS ALLURING? THIS MAKES MEN FAINT?! HA, HA!!

HA, HA! WELL, I HAVE TO STOP AT THE BANK BEFORE LUNCH-HOUR'S OVER!!

OKAY, HA, HA! SEE YOU BACK AT THE OFFICE!!

HERE, CATHY. MAY I TAKE YOUR SWEATER?

NO. IT'S PART OF THE OUTFIT.

IT SEEMS SO WARM.

IT IS NOT WARM.

YOU'LL BE UNCOMFORTABLE.

IRVING, THESE ARE SKIN-TIGHT STIRRUP PANTS, WHICH REVEAL EVERY RIPPLE FROM THE KNEE UP. THE SWEATER IS NOT COMING OFF!!

OH, COME ON. HOW BAD COULD THEY ...... I SEE.

HERE, CATHY. MAY I TAKE YOUR SWEATER?

NO. IT'S PART OF THE OUTFIT.

IF YOU'RE NOT HAPPY WITH THE PANTS, WHY DON'T YOU RETURN THEM, CATHY?

LIFE ISN'T THAT SIMPLE ANYMORE, MOM.

NOW IF I RETURN THE PANTS I ALSO HAVE TO DO SOMETHING WITH 2 SHIRTS, 4 BELTS, 3 CHUNKY NECKLACES, 14 SOCKS, A VEST, A SCARF, A WATCH, 4 PAIRS OF SHOES, AND A 7-PIECE DESK ORGANIZER SET I GOT TO GO WITH THEM.

YOU'RE KEEPING PANTS YOU DON'T LIKE FOR THAT??

IT'S EASIER TO STAY WITH THE PANTS THAN BREAK UP THE WHOLE FAMILY.

WHY SHOULDN'T I CALL MAX? I'M BEAUTIFUL! I'M BRIGHT! I'M CHARMING!

MAX!

OH, CATHY... I'M RUSHING TO GET A PLANE. I WAS GOING TO CALL YOU LATER IN THE WEEK, OKAY?

WHY DID I CALL MAX? I SOUNDED TOO EAGER. I SEEMED TOO AVAILABLE. WHY DID I HAVE TO CALL??

CONFIDENCE IS LIKE BATHING SUIT SEASON. IT ONLY LASTS LONG ENOUGH TO HUMILIATE ME.

WHEN IRVING AND I GOT REUNITED, WE SAID EVERYTHING WOULD BE DIFFERENT... IT WAS TOO DIFFERENT. WE MISSED THE OLD WAY WE WERE.

SO WE SAID, FINE. WE'LL BE THE OLD WAY... BUT IT WAS A NEW OLD WAY, NOT THE OLD OLD WAY.

WE SAID WE WANTED THE OLD ORIGINAL WAY, AND THAT SOMETIMES WE'D WANT THE NEW OLD WAY, AND SOMETIMES THE NEW NEW WAY AND SOMETIMES ALL DIFFERENT WAYS.

THIS ISN'T A RELATIONSHIP. IT'S A MINIATURE COCA-COLA COMPANY.

CATHY...UM..AHEM... THIS IS BRENDA AND...AHEM..HEH... UH, BRENDA, THIS IS CATHY....

TWO GIRLFRIENDS IN ONE ROOM! THEY'RE GOING TO KILL ME! THEY HATE ME!!

THEY MIGHT FORGIVE ME IN A YEAR... THEY MIGHT SPEAK TO ME IN A MONTH....BUT THERE IS NO DOUBT WHAT THEY'RE THINKING RIGHT NOW!!

HOW DOES MY HAIR LOOK?

IF WE WERE TWO MEN DATING THE SAME WOMAN, WE'D BE AT EACH OTHER'S THROATS... BUT HERE WE ARE, PRIMPING.

BRUSH BRUSH   ((POOF POOF))

MEN STRIKE OUT WITH SUCH BLATANT BLOWS. WOMEN COMPETE WITH SUBTLETY, DIGNITY AND FINESSE.

DAB BRUSH))   SQUIRT

IN FACT, THE MORE INTENSE THE COMPETITION, THE MORE WOMEN CALL UPON OUR OWN SPECIAL LANGUAGE OF ATTACK.

SQUIRT

36-C. WHAT ARE YOU??

I'M SORRY YOU HAD TO MEET BRENDA LIKE THAT, CATHY.

WHAT DO YOU SEE IN HER, IRVING??

I'M MORE TALENTED, MORE SUCCESSFUL AND MORE DEVOTED.

I HAVE MORE PASSION, MORE CHARISMA, MORE CHARM, MORE DEPTH, MORE HEART AND MORE OF THAT INDESCRIBABLE SOMETHING THAT SEPARATES THOSE DOOMED TO BE STRANGLED BY A LIFE OF FUTILE DREAMS FROM THOSE OF US WHO WILL BE STARS!

BRENDA SAID SHE THOUGHT YOU WERE "VERY NICE".

I'M ALSO MORE THOROUGH.

IF IRVING HAD MADE ME THIS MAD WHEN I WAS YOUNGER, I WOULD HAVE WRITTEN HIM A HIDEOUS LETTER AND THEN SPENT THE NIGHT BEATING MY FISTS ON THE MAILBOX, BEGGING TO GET IT BACK, MOM.

INSTEAD, I TOOK THAT SAME ENERGY AND PLANNED A HALLOWEEN PARTY.

THAT'S FANTASTIC, CATHY.

NEXT WEEK AT THIS TIME 45 PEOPLE WILL BE STANDING IN YOUR APARTMENT BECAUSE YOU TOOK THE INITIATIVE!

GIVE ME BACK MY INVITATIONS!!!

BAM BAM

U.S. MA

I SAW IRVING HAVING LUNCH WITH BRENDA, AND I'VE PLANNED A PARTY TO GET EVEN.

TO GET EVEN?

YES. I'M INVITING EVERY SINGLE MAN I KNOW AND TELLING THEM ALL TO COME AS DON JOHNSON. HAH!

IRVING HAD ONE LUNCH, AND YOU'RE STAGING A $500.00, 45-PERSON EXTRAVAGANZA SO YOU CAN SHATTER HIS CONFIDENCE, TRASH HIS EGO, AND TORTURE HIM WITH THE TYPE OF JEALOUSY FROM WHICH HE MAY NEVER RECOVER?

YES.

SOUNDS "EVEN" TO ME.

FLO AND I JUST HAD TO TAKE A PEEK AT WHAT YOU'VE PLANNED FOR YOUR HALLOWEEN PARTY, CATHY!

OH, IT'LL BE GREAT, MOM!

IRVING WILL WALK IN AND I'LL SLINK OVER LOOKING GORGEOUS AND SAY, "HA, HA, IRVING! MEET MAX!"... THEN GRANT WILL EMBRACE ME. I'LL SAY, "HA, HA, IRVING! MEET GRANT!"

THEN PAUL WILL COME UP. I'LL SAY, "HA, HA, MAX! MEET PAUL!"... "HA, HA, GRANT! MEET STEVE!"... "HA, HA, IRVING! MEET ED, BILL, AND JIM. HAH!"

SHOULDN'T YOU GET SOME CRACKERS OR SOMETHING?

FOR WHAT? NO ONE'S GOING TO BE HERE MORE THAN TWO MINUTES.

WHERE ARE ALL THE MEN, CATHY?

I'M SURE THE MEN WILL BE HERE.

YOU SAID THERE WOULD BE LOTS OF SINGLE MEN HERE. YOU PROMISED A GREAT RATIO!!

WE'VE ACTUALLY ACHIEVED THE TRADITIONAL HALLOWEEN PARTY RATIO, CHARLENE...

...25 CLEOPATRAS AND ONE GRAPE.

IRVING.... THIS IS MAX!

HI YA', BUDDY.

"HI YA', BUDDY"?? IRVING, A GORGEOUS MAN IS FEEDING ME GUACAMOLE WITH HIS BARE HANDS, AND ALL YOU CAN SAY IS, "HI YA', BUDDY"?!!

WHY NOT? I FIGURE HE'S JUST A PAL OF YOURS FROM WORK OR SOMETHING.

ISN'T THAT JUST LIKE A MAN TO JUMP TO THE WRONG CONCLUSIONS?

HOW WAS YOUR PARTY, CATHY?

IRVING AND MAX GOT ALONG SO WELL, THEY MADE PLANS TO PLAY RACQUETBALL, MOM.

TWENTY-FIVE WOMEN WHO WERE PREPARED TO GET DRUNK AND DO SOMETHING STUPID WOUND UP SITTING AROUND HAVING MEANINGFUL CONVERSATIONS WITH EACH OTHER.

THE FOOD WAS SUCH A SUCCESS THAT I DON'T HAVE ONE SINGLE THING LEFT TO RUIN MY DIET WITH.

HOW WAS CATHY'S PARTY?

IT WAS A DISASTER.

50

YOU WERE BRILLIANT IN THE MEETING, CATHY! BRILLIANT! CAN YOU LOOK AT THESE?

THANK YOU. YES! NO PROBLEM!

GREAT WORK, CATHY! THE REPORT WAS PERFECT! WILL YOU HANDLE THESE FOR ME?

THANK YOU. YES! OF COURSE!

MAGNIFICENT, CATHY! YOU'RE SO BRIGHT! YOU'RE SO EFFICIENT! WILL YOU....

...ONE DAY, WITHOUT WARNING, THE "PRAISE METHOD" LOSES ITS SNAP.

I'M SORRY YOU WERE UPSET ABOUT BRENDA LAST WEEK, CATHY...BUT I THOUGHT IT WAS GOOD FOR US TO SEE OTHER PEOPLE AND DO OTHER THINGS.

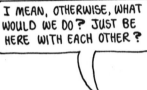

I MEAN, OTHERWISE, WHAT WOULD WE DO? JUST BE HERE WITH EACH OTHER?

AND THEN WHAT? YOU WANT ME TO SIT HERE SAYING, "I LOVE YOU, I LOVE YOU, I LOVE YOU" 24 HOURS A DAY? HA, HA! THAT WOULD BE RIDICULOUS!!

THE ONE TIME HE UNDERSTOOD ME, HE THOUGHT I WAS JOKING.

THIS LAYERED LOOK IS TOO YOUNG FOR ME, MOM.

NONSENSE, CATHY.

WHEN YOU LOOK YOUNG, YOU THINK YOUNG. WHEN YOU THINK YOUNG, YOU ACT YOUNG.

WHEN YOU ACT YOUNG, YOU SOUND YOUNG. AND WHEN YOU SOUND YOUNG, YOU'LL FEEL YOUNG FOREVER!!

I HAVE TO GO TO THE BATHROOM.

THIS LOOK IS TOO YOUNG FOR YOU.

AACK! MR. PINKLEY WANTS THIS BY NOON... BUT AAACK! I TOLD THE CLIENT HE'D HAVE THIS YESTERDAY!

...BUT AAAACK!! THIS HAS BEEN SITTING HERE FOR THREE WEEKS!!

WHY AREN'T YOU WORKING ON MY PROJECT, CATHY?

THERE COMES A TIME WHEN A PERSON HAS TO HEED HER OWN INNER VOICE, MR. PINKLEY.

YOUR CONSCIENCE?

MY AACK FACTOR.

HI, CHARLENE. THIS IS CATHY. I WON'T BE IN FOR THE REST OF THE AFTERNOON.

PRODUCT TESTING INC

RECEPTIONIST

DON'T TELL ME... YOU ATE A BIG DESSERT FOR LUNCH AND YOU FEEL TOO FAT TO COME BACK TO THE OFFICE.

I DID NOT EAT A BIG DESSERT.

I HAD A HAIR APPOINTMENT ON MY LUNCH HOUR, AND IT IS SIMPLY NOT POSSIBLE FOR ME TO MAKE IT BACK TO WORK.

IF ONE KIND OF MOUSSE DOESN'T GET YOU, THE OTHER KIND WILL.

WHEN A SOCIETY IS YOUNG, ALL PARTS OF IT HAVE TO BE TOTALLY FOCUSED ON COMMON GOALS IN ORDER TO SURVIVE...

BUT AFTER PROGRESS IS MADE, THE ACCOMPLISHMENTS ARE TAKEN FOR GRANTED, RULES ARE RELAXED, AND THE STAGE IS SET FOR RUIN.

I'M NOT JUST CHEATING ON MY DIET. I'M A CIVILIZATION ABOUT TO CRUMBLE.

53

I'VE DECIDED TO BUY A COMPUTER, CHARLENE.

YOU HAVE, CATHY?

YES. I HAVE THE BUG! I'VE BOUGHT THE CONCEPT! I WANT THE IMAGE! I'M WILLING! I'M READY! I'M SOLD! GET ME INTO THE '80s!! BRING ON MY COMPUTER!!!

WHAT DO YOU PLAN TO USE IT FOR?

WHAT HAPPENED?

HE GOT TOO TECHNICAL.

MAY I HELP YOU?

ME?..OH, NO... AHEM. NO.... THANK YOU...

DID YOU WANT TO SEE ANYTHING?

OH...AHEM...NO... JUST BROWSING. ..JUST *POINK!* AACK!...JUST BROWSING....

TAPPA TAPPA WHIRRR

LET ME KNOW IF YOU HAVE ANY QUESTIONS.

OH, NO. NO, THANK YOU. NO QUESTIONS. NO NEEDS. JUST PASSING THROUGH. AHEM...LOVELY SHOP. AHEM. THANK YOU AND GOOD DAY.

WHY DIDN'T YOU ASK ANYTHING, CATHY??

I DIDN'T WANT TO LOOK LIKE A BEGINNER.

COMPUTERS USED TO BE VERY INTIMIDATING, BUT NOW THE SOFTWARE IS SO USER-FRIENDLY!

THE SOFTWARE IS USER-FRIENDLY??

YES! WE HAVE THE 10-MEGABYTE CARD!

THE HARDWARE IS USER-FRIENDLY, TOO!

THE HARDWARE IS USER-FRIENDLY?

JUST PICK YOUR USER-FRIENDLY SOFTWARE, FIND USER-FRIENDLY HARDWARE WITH THE RAM AND, SAY, DOS VERSION TO SUPPORT IT AND, HA, HA! OF COURSE, THE INTERFACE TO CONVERT SIGNALS TO YOUR USER-FRIENDLY PERIPHERALS AND BOOM, YOU'RE THERE! CAN YOU BELIEVE IT?!!

NO.

EVERYBODY'S FRIENDLY, BUT NO ONE'S MAKING ANY SENSE.

YES! WE HAVE THE 10 MEGABYTE

LOTS OF PEOPLE BUY COMPUTERS, GET FRUSTRATED, AND THEN JUST STUFF THEM IN THE CLOSET, CATHY.

NOT I, MAX.

I COULDN'T STUFF A MAJOR PIECE OF EQUIPMENT LIKE THAT IN MY CLOSET!

MY VCR, FOOD PROCESSOR AND EXERCISE BIKE ARE TAKING UP ALL THE ROOM.

YOU'LL LOVE THIS... 16-BIT PROCESSOR WITH 256K EXPANDABLE TO 1 MEGABYTE, 2 RS-232 SERIAL PORTS, 8 EXPANSION SLOTS, PLASMA DISPLAY AND...

THANK YOU... YES. WELL, I MUST BE GOING.

SIZE 7! SIZE 7! BRING ME ANYTHING IN A SIZE 7!!

THERE'S NOTHING LIKE MEETING A STRANGER TO MAKE YOU APPRECIATE WHO YOU ALREADY LOVE.

I MAY GET A COMPUTER, CHARLENE, BUT I VOW TO NEVER GET THE SMIRK!

THE SMIRK?

YEAH... AS SOON AS PEOPLE KNOW THE FIRST THING ABOUT COMPUTERS THEY DEVELOP THIS SUPERIOR SMIRK THAT I JUST CAN'T STAND!

MAYBE IT'S SOMETHING IN THE SLOPPY DISKS.

"FLOPPY"... FOR HEAVEN'S SAKE, CHARLENE. THAT'S A FLOPPY DISK!

THAT WAS A SMIRK.

THAT WAS JUST A FLOPPY SMIRK. WAIT'LL YOU SEE HER HARD DISK SMIRK!

NOW YOU JUST MOVE THE LITTLE MOUSE AND POINT IT AT THE LITTLE HOUSE....

I'M ABOUT TO SPEND THOUSANDS OF DOLLARS ON A HIGHLY SOPHISTICATED MACHINE. I DO **NOT** NEED TO BE TREATED LIKE A CHILD!

FINE. EXIT TO THE SYSTEM AND LOG ONTO THE B DRIVE AT THE A: PROMPT WHERE YOU CAN RE-ENTER THE SPREADSHEED DIRECTORY AND REDEFINE PARAMETERS OF THE EXISTING FILE.

THANK YOU.

JUST MOVE THE LITTLE MOUSE AND POINT IT AT THE LITTLE HOUSE....

ATTENTION ALL EMPLOYEES: CATHY'S IN THE FINAL STAGE OF SELECTING A HOME COMPUTER.

ANY OF YOU WISHING TO TOTALLY CONFUSE HER WITH YOUR OWN OPINIONS OF WHAT TO BUY, STAND TO MY RIGHT...

...THOSE CLAIMING TO HAVE RELATIVES WHO CAN GET HER A DEAL, STAND TO MY LEFT.

THOSE WHO KNOW ZILCH ABOUT COMPUTERS, BUT FEEL LIKE EXPERTS BECAUSE THEY SAW THE MACINTOSH COMMERCIAL, STAND IN FRONT.

THERE'S NOTHING LIKE MAKING A MAJOR PURCHASE TO CONFIRM HOW MANY NERDS YOU WORK WITH.

..AND WHAT WOULD YOU BE USING A COMPUTER FOR?

THAT DOES IT.

EVERYWHERE I GO, I GET CONVINCED I NEED A COMPUTER, EXCEPT IN THE COMPUTER STORES, WHERE I HAVE TO KEEP EXPLAINING WHY I WANT ONE.

NORMAL PEOPLE CAN'T SHOP THAT WAY! NORMAL PEOPLE JUST WANT TO SPEND THE MONEY NOW AND BLAME THE SALESPERSON LATER! BLEAH TO YOU AND BLEAH TO YOUR WHOLE GIZMO FACTORY!!!

WHAT DID **THAT** ACCOMPLISH??

IT HELPED NARROW DOWN THE NUMBER OF STORES WHERE I MAY BE MAKING MY PURCHASE.

Panel 1: THERE COMES A TIME IN A RELATIONSHIP WHEN A COUPLE NEEDS TO START SPENDING HOLIDAYS TOGETHER, IRVING.

Panel 2: IT'S A SHOW OF LOVE... A VOTE OF UNITY... THE FINAL TRANSITION TO ADULTHOOD!

Panel 3: MAYBE YOU'RE RIGHT...YOU WANT TO FLY HOME WITH ME FOR THANKSGIVING, CATHY?

Panel 4: NO... I'M READY FOR YOU TO BE AN ADULT. I'M NOT READY FOR ME TO BE AN ADULT.

Panel 5: I GUESS I COULD ASK MOM ABOUT HAVING THANKSGIVING WITH YOUR PARENTS INSTEAD OF MINE, IRVING.
THERE'S NO HARM IN ASKING, CATHY.

Panel 6: WE'LL STOP BY HER HOUSE AND I'LL JUST SAY....UH OH.
WHAT? UH OH WHAT?

Panel 7: GO BACK! TURN THE CAR AROUND! FORGET IT! I'M HAVING THANKSGIVING AT HER HOUSE AND THAT'S THAT!!
WE'RE STILL A BLOCK FROM HER STREET.

Panel 8: MOTHERLY INTUITION: NOW BEAMED BY SATELLITE.

Panel 9: FLO NEKERVIS IS HAVING 5 DAUGHTERS, 3 SONS-IN-LAW AND 4 GRANDCHILDREN FOR THANKSGIVING.
IRVING MIGHT BE JOINING US, MOM.

Panel 10: FLO'S BORROWING CHAIRS, RENTING CRIBS AND STORING FOOD IN MY REFRIGERATOR.
IRVING MIGHT BE GUILT-RIDDEN FOR NOT BEING WITH HIS OWN FAMILY.

Panel 11: IRVING MIGHT BE PARANOID, ACT WEIRD, AND JUST PLANT HIMSELF IN FRONT OF THE FOOTBALL GAME ON TV FOR FOUR HOURS.

Panel 12: YOU MAY BE MAKING SIX PIES, FLO, BUT CATHY'S BRINGING A 170-POUND TURKEY.

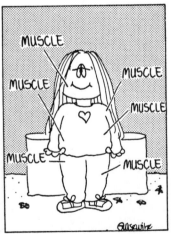

GOOD MORNING AND WELCOME TO EVERY EMPLOYER'S NIGHTMARE: DECEMBER.

FOR ONCE, THIS OFFICE IS NOT GOING TO DETERIORATE INTO A HOLIDAY GOSSIP CENTER, PARTY HEADQUARTERS OR FRUITCAKE EMPORIUM.

WE WILL REMAIN IN DECEMBER WHAT WE'VE WORKED SO HARD TO BECOME THE OTHER 11 MONTHS OF THE YEAR!

A PLACE WHERE WE CAN STOP AND USE THE LADIES ROOM IN BETWEEN SHOPPING.

TONIGHT? NO. I CANNOT WORK LATE TONIGHT, MR. PINKLEY.

IRVING HAD TO WORK LATE ALL LAST WEEK AND I HAVE A BIG SELF-RIGHTEOUS SPEECH PLANNED FOR TONIGHT.

IF I HAVE TO WORK LATE IT RUINS EVERYTHING! IT UPSETS THE WHOLE BALANCE OF EQUALITY!

IT WAS YOUR TURN TO COOK DINNER?

IT WAS MY TURN TO HAVE THE TANTRUM!!

MISS! I'VE BEEN STANDING HERE FOR FIVE MINUTES!

WHEN I TRIED TO HELP YOU TEN MINUTES AGO, YOU SAID I WAS BEING TOO PUSHY.

BAM BAM!

IF I LEAVE YOU ALONE, YOU FEEL IGNORED. IF I PAY ATTENTION TO YOU, YOU FEEL SUFFOCATED!!'

WELL, I'VE HAD IT! GET OUT OF HERE! I'M SICK OF TRYING TO GUESS WHAT WILL MAKE YOU HAPPY!!!

MY RELATIONSHIPS MAY BE BRIEF, BUT THEY ARE NEVER WITHOUT PASSION.

DO YOU REMEMBER THE DR. ATKINS DIET, CATHY?

BLEAH! THAT WAS THE WORST!!

...NO..WAIT...FOR THREE WEEKS IN 1972 I ATE NOTHING BUT HARD-BOILED EGGS AND GRAPE-FRUIT! THAT WAS THE WORST!

WAIT... HOW ABOUT PINEAPPLE DAY ON THE BEVERLY HILLS DIET?! HALF THE OFFICE WENT HOME EARLY!!

YES! OR METRECAL! BLEAH! CANNED METRECAL!

WE REMINISCE ABOUT OUR DIETS LIKE SOME PEOPLE REMINISCE ABOUT THEIR VACATIONS.

LAST YEAR EVERYONE CHARGED OUT OF THE OFFICE AT 4:30 TO GO CHRISTMAS SHOPPING... THIS YEAR PEOPLE ARE STILL WORKING AT 7:00 AT NIGHT.

THE WORK ETHIC IS BACK! PRIDE IS BACK!

PEOPLE HAVE FINALLY DISCOVERED THERE'S NO LIMIT TO WHAT CAN BE GAINED IF THEY JUST STAY AT THOSE DESKS!!

I WANT THE COFFEE GRINDER ON PAGE 42...THE SHOWER-RADIO ON PAGE 108...THE NECKTIE ON PAGE 75....

DO YOU WANT A GIFT BOX, OR IS THIS LACE BODY STOCKING FOR YOURSELF?

AHEM... A GIFT BOX! OF COURSE I WANT A GIFT BOX!

THIS WOMAN WANTS A BOX FOR HER LACE BODY STOCKING.

A GIFT BOX. IT IS A GIFT, SO I NEED A NICE GIFT BOX.

ANYONE KNOW IF WE HAVE A BOX FOR HER LACE BODY STOCKING?!

NEVER MIND. I DON'T NEED A BOX. JUST STUFF IT IN THE BAG. I DO NOT NEED A BOX!!

WHY JUST MAKE A SALE WHEN YOU CAN CREATE A RETAIL EVENT?

WHEN THE MARY TYLER MOORE SHOW WENT OFF THE AIR, I FELT SO DESERTED AND ALONE. HOW COULD SHE LEAVE WHEN I NEEDED HER SO MUCH??

NOW, AFTER FORCING ME TO COPE ON MY OWN FOR 7 YEARS, SHE'S WALTZING BACK ONTO MY TV SET TONIGHT, TRYING TO START IT ALL OVER WITH A WHOLE NEW SHOW.

WHEW! I CAN IMAGINE HOW YOU FEEL, CATHY.

YOU'RE BACK! WELCOME BACK! OH, THANK HEAVENS, MARY, YOU FINALLY CAME BACK!!

IT'S ALWAYS HARD TO EXPLAIN THE REUNION TO SOMEONE WHO WASN'T IN THE RELATIONSHIP.

64

I THOUGHT YOU WERE DOING ALL YOUR SHOPPING BY CATALOG THIS YEAR, CATHY.

I STARTED TO, BUT IT JUST DIDN'T SEEM RIGHT.

FOR HIM   FOR HER   FOR

CHRISTMAS IS SUCH A SPECIAL TIME. I FELT I WAS MISSING SOMETHING VERY MEANINGFUL BY JUST ORDERING OVER THE PHONE.

R HIM   FOR HE

I KNOW...YOU CAN'T REALLY SEE WHAT YOU'RE BUYING.

OH, IT WAS MUCH DEEPER THAN THAT, CHARLENE.

I COULDN'T SEE THE SALESCLERK I WAS SCREAMING AT.

HOW DID YOU GET THIS REPORT DONE SO FAST, CATHY?!

I PROMISED MYSELF A PAIR OF PINK SUEDE BOOTS, MR. PINKLEY.

I PROMISED MYSELF A BLUE ANGORA SWEATER FOR THE CLEMENT PROJECT...A LONG BLACK SKIRT FOR THE ROSEN PROJECT AND ONE PAIR OF GLIMMERY PANTYHOSE FOR EACH AND EVERY IDIOTIC MEMO.

WORKING FOR YOU TODAY HAS COST ME A POTENTIAL $425.

IT'S BEGINNING TO LOOK A LOT LIKE CHRISTMAS BONUS TIME.

LOOK AT THIS GREAT PHONE I PICKED UP AT THE DRUGSTORE, CATHY!

WHAT?? YOU GOT YOURSELF A PHONE?

I'VE BEEN SEARCHING ALL WEEK FOR THE PERFECT PHONE TO GET YOU FOR CHRISTMAS, AND YOU WANDERED OUT AND BOUGHT ONE FOR YOURSELF?!!

WHAT IS THE MATTER WITH YOU?? HAVE YOU NO SELF-CONTROL?! HAVE YOU NO IMAGINATION??

SHE BOUGHT HIM A GIFT, AND NOW SHE'S LETTING HIM HAVE IT.

BONK!

HOW ABOUT THIS NICE SHIRT FOR YOUR BOY-FRIEND?

NO. THERE ARE TOO MANY OF THEM. I'M AFRAID EVERYONE WILL HAVE THOSE.

HOW ABOUT A SWEATER VEST?

NO. THE DISPLAY IS TOO PROMINENT. HE'LL KNOW WHERE I BOUGHT IT AND HOW MUCH IT COST.

SPECIAL $19.99

I'VE SEEN TOO MANY COMMER-CIALS FOR THESE, TOO MANY CATALOGS ON THESE, AND TOO MANY STORES WITH THESE.

WHAT IS IT YOU'RE LOOK-ING FOR?

DO YOU HAVE ANYTHING THAT'S HIDDEN?

MY FRIENDS ARE ALL STARTING TO PUT PICTURES OF THEIR GRANDCHIL-DREN ON THEIR CHRISTMAS CARDS.

ARE YOU JEALOUS, MOM?

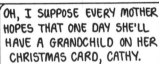

OH, I SUPPOSE EVERY MOTHER HOPES THAT ONE DAY SHE'LL HAVE A GRANDCHILD ON HER CHRISTMAS CARD, CATHY.

YOU CAN WRITE LETTERS TO YOUR FRIENDS...YOU CAN CALL.....BUT NOTHING QUITE SAYS WHAT A PICTURE OF YOUR OWN GRANDCHILD SAYS.

"MY CHILDREN ARE NORMAL."

RETAILERS BREATHED A HUGE SIGH OF RELIEF TODAY AS CHRISTMAS SALES FINALLY SHOT UPWARD....

UH, OH. I HAVE TO CALL THE NEWS, MOM.

FOR WHAT, CATHY?

I BOUGHT ALL KINDS OF THINGS TODAY THAT I'M GOING TO RETURN. THE RE-TAILERS NEED TO BE WARNED!!

DON'T BE RIDICULOUS. HOW MUCH COULD ONE PERSON'S "RETURN" PILE AFFECT THE ECONOMIC PICTURE OF THE ENTIRE COUNTRY?!

CALL THE NEWS.

IS CATHY IN? I WANT TO GO OVER SOME NEW FIGURES WITH HER.

WHAT?? IT'S TWO DAYS BEFORE CHRISTMAS!

WHO CARES ABOUT YOUR STUPID FIGURES?? WHO CARES ABOUT YOUR WHOLE STUPID COMPANY??

AND WHAT DO YOU MEAN BOTHERING US HERE AT THE OFFICE WHILE I'M TRYING TO FINISH MY GIFT WRAPPING?!!!

BAM BAM

ANY MESSAGES, CHARLENE?

NO. NO ONE'S LEAVING ANY MESSAGES TODAY.

"I AM AN ADULT, MOTHER, AND THIS YEAR I WILL RELATE TO YOU ONLY AS AN ADULT!"

CATHY, MY BABY! YOU'RE HERE! SHE'S HERE! TAKE A PICTURE ...MAKE A TAPE! LOOK! SHE'S SMILING!!

EAT! YOU MUST BE STARVING! NO...SLEEP! YOU MUST BE EXHAUSTED! NO...WAKE UP! I WANT TO SEE YOU, OH, YOU'RE BEAUTIFUL, LET ME LOOK AT YOU, LET ME HOLD YOU!

OH, MY SWEET BABY, YOU'VE COME HOME FOR CHRISTMAS!

POINK

CHRISTMAS DINNER WAS WONDERFUL!

I CAN'T MOVE.

I'M STUFFED.

HERE... I'LL CLEAR THE TABLE, CATHY.

NO, THANKS, DAD. IT'S SORT OF A SPECIAL TRADITION FOR MOM AND ME TO CLEAN UP AFTER HOLIDAY DINNERS.

THERE'S NO WAY A MAN COULD UNDERSTAND WHAT GOES ON IN THE KITCHEN AFTER A MEAL OF THIS MAGNITUDE!

EAT CHOMP EAT CHOMP EAT CHOMP

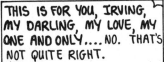

THIS IS FOR YOU, IRVING, MY DARLING, MY LOVE, MY ONE AND ONLY.... NO. THAT'S NOT QUITE RIGHT.

MERRY CHRISTMAS, YOU SEXY HUNK, YOU INCREDIBLE MAN, YOU GORGEOUS....NO. THAT'S NOT QUITE RIGHT....

HERE'S A LITTLE SOMETHING I GRABBED FOR YOU, IRV... .. HA, HA! LOVE YA!'....NO. THAT'S NOT QUITE RIGHT...

CATHY, YOU'VE SPENT MORE TIME FIGURING OUT THE SPEECH THAN THE GIFT.

THE SPEECH IS HARDER TO TAKE BACK.

WE WILL GO STRAIGHT TO THE RETURN DESK... WE WILL GO STRAIGHT TO THE RETURN DESK...

WE WILL BUY NOTHING... LOOK AT NOTHING... TRY ON NOTHING...

TOUCH NOTHING! PICK UP NOTHING! MODEL NOTHING! BRING HOME NOTHING!

WHEN THE SONG IS SO FAMILIAR, YOU QUIT PAYING ATTENTION TO THE WORDS.

I HAVE TO GO BACK TO WORK THIS MORNING, MOM.

DON'T BE RIDICULOUS, CATHY. YOU JUST GOT HERE!

I CAN'T STAY.

OF COURSE YOU'LL STAY.

I HAVE TO WORK.

YOU'LL STAY AND EAT.

I'LL EAT BUT I CAN'T STAY!

YOU'LL EAT AND STAY!

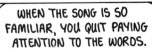

MOTHER'S COOKING: THE ORIGINAL POWER BREAKFAST.

THUNK!

Z Z Z Z Z Z

WHY IS EVERYONE STILL HERE? THE BROWN WRAPPING PAPER IS ALL USED UP... THE TAPE IS ALL GONE...THE POSTAGE METER IS EMPTY AND ALL THE RED FELT-TIP PENS ARE DRY.

MR. PINKLEY, YOUR STAFF DOES NOT JUST STAY LATE TO PILFER SUPPLIES!

SORRY, CATHY. I GUESS I UNDER-ESTIMATED YOU.

YOU MOST CERTAINLY DID.

WE'RE HAVING A CONTEST TO SEE WHO CAN CHARGE THE MOST LONG-DISTANCE CALLS TO THE COMPANY BEFORE THE NEW YEAR.

DO THESE SPARKLES MAKE MY LEGS LOOK SKINNY OR DO THEY JUST MAKE THE FAT TWINKLE?

DOES THIS DRESS MAKE ME LOOK SULTRY OR CHEAP?...WILL THE PLASTIC JEWELRY DRIVE IRVING WILD WITH PASSION...OR WILL IT MAKE HIM SAY, "SHE'S WEARING PLASTIC JEWELRY"?

THE SPARKLES... THE DRESS.. ...THE PLASTIC.

IF YOU CAN'T WEAR YOUR GRAND ILLUSIONS FOR THE HOLIDAYS, WHEN CAN YOU WEAR THEM?

SIX STRAIGHT HOURS OF FOOTBALL AND YOU HAVEN'T RUN FROM THE ROOM SCREAMING YET.

THIS IS THE FIRST DAY OF A NEW YEAR, IRVING.

DON'T YOU KNOW WHY I'M HERE?? DON'T YOU KNOW WHY I'D WANT TO SPEND THE FIRST DAY OF THE WHOLE YEAR SITTING BY YOUR SIDE?

THE STORES AREN'T OPEN.

I GAINED AND LOST THE SAME FIVE POUNDS ALL LAST YEAR, CHARLENE.

ONE WEEK I'D GAIN IT... ONE WEEK I'D LOSE IT. NO BIG DEAL.

NOW I'VE LAUNCHED AN ALL-OUT EFFORT TO LOSE **TWENTY** POUNDS, AND SUDDENLY I CAN'T EVEN GET AN OUNCE OF THE ORIGINAL FIVE POUNDS TO BUDGE.

AS SOON AS THEY KNOW YOU'RE SERIOUS ABOUT BREAK-ING UP, THEY WON'T LET GO.

I THOUGHT YOU WEREN'T GOING TO EAT ANY PIE UN-TIL YOU LOST TEN POUNDS, CATHY.

I'M NOT. I'M JUST EVENING OFF THE EDGES.

IT LOOKS TO ME LIKE YOU'RE EATING PIE.

I'M NOT. I'M JUST SMOOTHING THE SIDES.

I'M STRAIGHTENING OUT THE ANGLE... GETTING THE LEFT SIDE TO MATCH THE RIGHT... TRIMMING THE EXTRA CRUST... CLEANING OUT THE CRUMBS...

CAN'T YOU SEE WHAT YOU'RE DOING ??

YES. I'M MAKING SURE ONE THING IN THE HOUSE IS NEAT.

BEFORE

SCRAPE SHOVEL SCRAPE DIG CHIP DIG SCRAPE

AFTER

YESTERDAY, THE INSTANT MAKEOVER. TODAY, THE AUTO MAKEOVER.

FINE. **DON'T** START. WHO NEEDS YOU, YOU MISERABLE PILE OF RUST ?!!

CLICK.

...WAIT.....I DIDN'T MEAN IT...PLEASE START ONE MORE TIME... I'LL DO ANYTHING....

YOU PATHETIC EXCUSE FOR TRANSPORTATION! YOU DISGUSTING JUNK HEAP! YOU WORTHLESS DUMPSTER!

BAM BAM

..WAAH! GIVE ME ONE MORE CHANCE! I'M BEGGING YOU!

THERE'S NOTHING LIKE WATCHING ANOTHER COUPLE TO MAKE YOU FEEL GOOD ABOUT YOUR OWN RELATIONSHIP.

WAIT... LET ME GET THE GARBAGE OUT OF THE BACK SEAT!

...LET ME SCRAPE THE FRENCH FRIES OFF THE FLOOR ...LET ME STICK THE MIRROR BACK ON...LET ME PRY THE GUM OUT OF THE ASHTRAY.....

THIS KLUNKER IS SO FAR GONE IT WON'T EVEN START. WHAT DO YOU CARE IF THE SERVICE DEPARTMENT SEES FRENCH FRIES ON THE FLOOR ?!

I DON'T WANT THEM TO THINK I HAVEN'T BEEN TAKING NICE CARE OF IT.

HERE, LITTLE LADY...YOUR CARBURETOR'S SHOT, CAUSING GASKET LEAKS ON THE ALTERNATOR DRIVE SHAFT SLIP YOKE CYLINDER HEAD NUTS. OBVIOUSLY, THIS ALL HAS TO GO.

SEE ??

YES, I SEE. THAT IS THE EXACT SAME TWITCH IRVING GETS IN HIS EYE WHEN HIS "SEMINAR" IS REALLY A WEEKEND WITH BRENDA.

EITHER COME UP WITH AN ESTIMATE THAT DOESN'T MAKE YOU SQUINT, OR I'M TOWING THIS KLUNKER ELSEWHERE !!

I KNOW NOTHING ABOUT CARS, BUT I KNOW A LOT ABOUT EYELIDS.

73

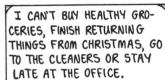

YOUR WARRANTY COVERS THE MAJOR PART, BUT IT DOESN'T SEEM TO COVER THE LITTLE #200 TUBE LEADING TO THE PART.

MY WARRANTY DOESN'T COVER THE LITTLE #200 TUBE??

NO. SEE THE FINE PRINT? "THE LITTLE #200 TUBE IS NOT COVERED ON 2-DOOR 1984 MODELS PURCHASED IN JUNE."

LET ME SEE THIS LITTLE #200 TUBE!!

OH, I'M NOT SURE WE HAVE ANY LITTLE TUBES.

YOU'VE HAD MY CAR FOR A WEEK AND YOU HAVEN'T EVEN STARTED **LOOKING** FOR THE LITTLE TUBE??!!

DON'T BE RIDICULOUS. IT TOOK US THIS LONG TO FIND THE LITTLE LOOPHOLE.

HELLO??...I'VE BEEN ON HOLD FOR THE SERVICE DEPARTMENT FOR TEN MINUTES...HELLO?? WHERE IS EVERYONE?!

WHY WON'T YOU TALK TO ME? COME BACK HERE! DON'T LEAVE ME STRANDED IN NEVER-NEVER LAND!!

...OH, YEAH?? WELL, BLEAH! AHA! TAKE THAT!

SLAM

SOMETIMES IT SEEMS LIKE THE ONLY POWER I HAVE IN MY RELATIONSHIPS IS TO BREAK UP.

MY CAR'S STILL IN THE SHOP, CHARLENE...I WANT YOU TO DRIVE ME TO THE MALL AT LUNCHTIME.....I'LL BUY A SLINKY DRESS...TAKE A CAB TO THE GROCERY STORE....

...SWING PAST THE FLORIST'S... GRAB A BUS TO MY APARTMENT...SET UP A ROMANTIC CANDLELIGHT DINNER...BEG MY LANDLADY TO TAKE ME TO THE BEAUTY PARLOR...

...SEND A MESSENGER TO THE WINE AND CHEESE SHOP...AND THEN HAVE MOM SHOOT ME OVER TO BUY SOME MOOD MUSIC ON MY WAY BACK TO THE OFFICE FOR MY 2:00 MEETING!!

RING RING

...OH, HI, IRVING. YOU'LL HAVE TO COME TO MY PLACE TONIGHT, SWEETIE. I DON'T HAVE A CAR.

I DIDN'T KNOW HOW YOU TWO WOULD REACT TO ME BEING PREGNANT, CATHY.

SHE DIDN'T KNOW HOW WE'D REACT, MOM!

OH, ANDREA, EVERY WOMAN IN HISTORY HAS PROBABLY REACTED TO THE NEWS OF A PREGNANCY THE SAME!!

YEAH, I GUESS YOU'RE RIGHT.

...LET'S SEE...SHE GOT MARRIED IN SEPTEMBER...SHE'S DUE IN JUNE...THAT'S 7...8..8½...

I NEVER FORGAVE YOU FOR GETTING MARRIED LAST SUMMER, ANDREA. YOU WERE MY BEST FRIEND...MY FOUNDATION....AND YOU JUST DISAPPEARED.

LUKE AND I NEEDED SOME TIME TOGETHER, CATHY, BUT I'M BACK NOW.

YOU'RE MARRIED AND PREGNANT NOW. WE CAN'T HAVE THE KIND OF FRIENDSHIP WE USED TO.

OF COURSE WE CAN.

NO, ANDREA. YOU HAD A SPECIAL PLACE IN MY LIFE THAT YOU CAN NEVER FILL AGAIN...

...YOU WERE GOING TO BE THE OLD MAID!!

CARRYING THIS BABY IS THE RICHEST EXPERIENCE OF MY LIFE!

THAT DOES IT, ANDREA. I MET YOU WHEN I WAS YOUNG AND CUTE AND YOU SPENT TEN YEARS CONVINCING ME TO FORGO MY RELATIONSHIPS FOR MY CAREER.

NOW I'M OLD AND FAT AND WRINKLED AND ALL THE MEN ARE MARRIED...AND NOW YOU SAY I WON'T BE FULFILLED IF I DON'T EXPERIENCE CHILDBEARING!

WHY WASN'T I WARNED?! HOW COULD YOU GO OFF AND DECIDE THIS WITHOUT ME?!!

SORRY, CATHY. I GUESS WE SORT OF LOST TOUCH.

WHEN SOME PEOPLE LOSE TOUCH THEY MISS A BIRTHDAY. I KEEP MISSING WHOLE ERAS.

MAYBE AUNT CATHY WILL COME WITH...

HOLD IT, ANDREA. IF YOU THINK YOU CAN WIN ME OVER TO THE IDEA OF YOUR PREGNANCY BY MAKING ME A "RELATIVE," YOU'RE WRONG.

YOU MET MR. WONDERFUL. YOU MARRIED MR. WONDERFUL. YOU'RE HAVING A BABY WITH MR. WONDERFUL.

YOU ARE NOT GOING TO GLOSS OVER MY INNER TURMOIL AND ENDEAR ME TO PARENTING BY HAVING YOUR BABY CALL ME AUNT CATHY!!

OH MY GOD.

LOOK! UNCLE IRVING HAS DROPPED BY TO SEE YOU!

SOME PEOPLE SAY THE NEW "MATERNITY LOOK" IN CLOTHES IS SO POPULAR BECAUSE ALL THE FRUSTRATED SINGLE WOMEN WANT TO PRETEND THEY'RE PREGNANT.

THAT'S LUDICROUS.

I AM A SERIOUS, FASHION-CONSCIOUS BUSINESSWOMAN! I DO NOT WEAR THE LATEST STYLES BECAUSE I'M TRYING TO PRETEND I'M PREGNANT!!

I'M TRYING TO PRETEND I DIDN'T EAT 23 MACADAMIA-NUT COOKIES ON THE WAY HOME FROM THE OFFICE LAST NIGHT.

WANT TO CATCH A MOVIE WITH US TONIGHT, ANDREA?

YES! THE POPCORN WOULD BE AN EXCELLENT FIBER SOURCE TO HELP KEEP MOMMY'S DIGESTIVE TRACT FREE OF TOXINS.

THE DOLBY SOUND ON HUGE SPEAKERS WOULD BE A WONDERFUL SENSORY EVENT FOR THE BABY, AND SITTING AND SHIFTING IN MY SEAT WILL CAUSE WAVES IN THE AMNIOTIC SAC, STIMULATING BABY'S ARM AND LEG MOVEMENT.

YES! A MOVIE WOULD BE A FINE PRENATAL EXPERIENCE, ESPECIALLY AFTER 8:00PM, WHEN THE FETUS IS MOST RESPONSIVE TO INFANT STIMULATION!!

IT'S MORE THAN A PREGNANCY. IT'S A RELIGION.

IT'S TYPICAL FOR WOMEN WHO HAVE BEEN REAL GO-GETTERS IN BUSINESS TO TURN THAT SAME PASSION ONTO THE EXPERIENCE OF PARENTING.

SOME START WITH FLASH CARDS AND MUSIC LESSONS WHEN THEIR BABY IS JUST A WEEK OLD. YOU'RE NOT GOING TO DO THAT ARE YOU, ANDREA?

START EDUCATING THE BABY A WEEK AFTER BIRTH?? DON'T BE RIDICULOUS.

WE WOULD HAVE MISSED THE WHOLE NINE MONTHS OF PREGNANCY!

..THIS NEXT SELECTION IS FROM VIVALDI, LITTLE ONE...

HELLO, BABY. THIS IS MOMMY. PAT. PAT. MOMMY PATS BABY.

YOU'RE TALKING TO YOUR UNBORN CHILD THROUGH A PAPER TOWEL TUBE?

IT'S ONE OF THE FIRST SIMPLE LESSONS IN OUR "AVANT-BIRTH" COURSE, CATHY.

I THOUGHT YOU DIDN'T BELIEVE IN PUSHING FOR A "SUPER BABY."

"SUPER BABY." OF COURSE NOT. WE'RE NOT TRYING TO HAVE A "SUPER BABY."

WE'RE GOING FOR GENIUS!! WE WANT A GENIUS!!

HELLO, BABY. THAT WAS DADDY. DADDY WAS JUST JOKING. HA, HA. SAY HA, HA, DADDY.

HA, HA.

OH, LUKE...I WANT THIS BABY TO HAVE ALL THE THINGS WE NEVER HAD.

YEAH...

SNIFF

WHAT'S WRONG, ANDREA?

I CAN'T THINK OF ANYTHING WE'VE NEVER HAD.

80

I DON'T GET IT, CATHY. HOW IS ANDREA SO SURE SHE WANTS TO BE PREGNANT??

SHE'S OLDER THAN WE ARE, CHARLENE.

BUT HOW DOES SHE REALLY **KNOW**?? HOW COULD SHE MAKE THAT KIND OF COMMITMENT?!

SHE'S OLDER.

SHE'S OLDER.

YEAH, YOU'RE RIGHT. SHE'S OLDER.

SHE'S OLDER.

SHE'S ONLY SIX MONTHS OLDER.

SIX MONTHS IS A LONG TIME IN THE WORLD OF BABIES.

LOOK, DEAR...THERE'S ANDREA AND THERE'S HER BABY! HI, BABY!

HI, BABY!

MAYBE WE CAN FEEL THE BABY KICKING!

I HAVEN'T FELT A BABY KICK SINCE YOU WERE PREGNANT WITH CATHY!

I CAN'T WAIT UNTIL WE CAN HOLD THE BABY!!

WE LOVE BABIES!

OH, HOORAY, WE'RE GOING TO KNOW A BABY!

WE WANT TO HOLD A BABY!

CAN WE BABY-SIT?!

ARE YOUR PARENTS OK, CATHY??

YEAH...THEIR BIOLOGICAL GRANDFATHER CLOCK JUST WENT OFF.

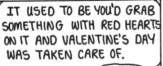

IT USED TO BE YOU'D GRAB SOMETHING WITH RED HEARTS ON IT AND VALENTINE'S DAY WAS TAKEN CARE OF.

YEAH.

NOW THERE ARE A MILLION SHAPES AND SIZES OF EVERY-THING... HOW DO I KNOW WHAT SHE'LL THINK IS SEXY? HOW DO I KNOW WHAT'S "ROMAN-TIC AND FUN" AND WHAT WILL TOTALLY OFFEND HER??

AND HOW AM I SUPPOSED TO PICK ANYTHING OUT WITH ALL THOSE PEOPLE LOOKING AT ME?!

YEAH, I KNOW. LINGERIE'S A PRETTY PERSONAL THING.

WHAT LINGERIE? I'M TALKING ABOUT A GREETING CARD.

IRVING SENT ME ROSES FOR VALENTINE'S DAY, MOM. AND A WONDERFUL CARD! AND TICKETS TO A PLAY!

ROSES! OH, CATHY! A CARD! A PLAY!

ISN'T HE PERFECT?!

OH, YES. HOW PERFECT. HOW THOUGHTFUL.

WHAT A HUNK. WHAT A HERO. WHAT A PRIZE! OH, MY GOODNESS. WOW. WHAT A GUY!

NO RING.

IRVING SENT THESE??

YEAH...AREN'T THEY BEAUTIFUL?

I THINK SEEING THE TOWN FILLED WITH ROMANTIC CARDS AND GIFTS HELPED HIM FEEL OK ABOUT EXPRESSING HIMSELF.

EVEN THE MOST UNSENTIMENTAL MEN IN THE WORLD MUST FEEL THE SAME THING AT THE END OF THIS WEEK!

THANK GOD I LIVED THROUGH ANOTHER VALENTINE'S DAY!

I THOUGHT YOU WERE HAVING LUNCH WITH IRVING, CATHY.

NO, I'M NOT HAVING LUNCH WITH IRVING.

IRVING DECIDED TO PLAY RACQUETBALL AT LUNCH.

IRVING WOULD RATHER RUN AROUND A LITTLE ROOM GETTING ALL SWEATY WITH SOME NERDY FRIEND THAN HAVE A NICE LUNCH WITH ME!!!

BAM SMACK BAM

HE ACTS LIKE A PIG AND I BECOME ONE.

84

"WRITE ON, WIPE OFF." "STICK DOWN, PEEL UP"

"SNAP OFF".."FLIP OFF"..."LIFT OFF"..."POP OFF"... "TOSS OUT"... "TEAR OPEN"..."POP UP".."THROW OUT"..."SNIP OFF"... "POUR OUT"...

"DISSOLVES"..."DISAPPEARS".. "VANISHES"..."EVAPORATES".. "FLUSHES".."DRAINS"..."WIPES".. .."WHISKS"..., "ZIPS AWAY"..

SOMETIMES I FEEL LIKE I'M THE ONLY THING IN THIS APARTMENT THAT ISN'T ABOUT TO GO SOMEPLACE.

YOU NEVER SAY, "I LOVE YOU," IRVING. WHY CAN'T YOU JUST SAY, "I LOVE YOU"?

OOPS... HANG ON... THERE'S THE PHONE.

RING RING!

HI, IRVING? THIS IS STACEY. I..UH... I'M IN YOUR AERO-BICS CLASS.

AHEM... OH, HI. HI!

I...WELL, I THINK YOU'RE GORGEOUS AND I WONDERED IF YOU'D LIKE TO GO OUT TOMORROW.

ME? AHEM... WELL, YES. GREAT. YES.

I LOVE YOU, CATHY!!

UH OH.

I'VE WORKED LATE AND LOOK FABULOUS... I SHOULD DROP BY AND SEE IRVING ON MY WAY HOME.

MY HAIR IS PERFECT, MY CLOTHES ARE ADORABLE...I'LL JUST POP OVER AND SURPRISE HIM WITH MY RUMPLED BEAUTY.

APART BUILD

I'LL JUST RING THE BELL, BAT MY LOVELY EYES AND SAY....

THE BETTER I LOOK, THE MORE INCLINED I AM TO DO SOMETHING STUPID.

WHO IS SHE AND WHAT'S SHE DOING AT IRVING'S APARTMENT?!

IRVING DIDN'T MENTION HER... IRVING DIDN'T EVEN HINT THAT HE WAS SEEING ANYONE ELSE.

WHAT KIND OF LOW, SCUMMY MAN WOULD LET ME THINK I WAS THE ONLY ONE IN HIS LIFE?!!

FUNNY HOW ALL THE WOMEN I DATE HAVE SORT OF THE SAME LOOK TO THEM.

CATHY, THIS IS STACEY. STACEY CALLED ME UP AND ASKED ME OUT TONIGHT. I'M INNOCENT.

STACEY, THIS IS CATHY. CATHY DROPPED OVER ON HER OWN WITH NO WARNING. I'M INNOCENT.

I AM TOTALLY INNOCENT! TWO WOMEN ARE PURSUING ME AND I AM ABSOLUTELY INNOCENT! FOR ONCE IN MY LIFE, I'M INNOCENT, INNOCENT, INNOCENT!!!

HOO BOY. DO I FEEL GUILTY.

SHE ASKED ME OUT AND I WENT OUT. DO YOU HAVE TO MAKE SUCH A BIG DEAL OUT OF IT TONIGHT?

NO.

I CAN MAKE A BIG DEAL OUT OF IT NOW AND GET IT OVER WITH...

...OR I CAN PRETEND EVERYTHING IS FINE NOW AND SPEND THE NEXT SIX MONTHS PLOTTING AND SCHEMING A WEB OF REVENGE SO HIDEOUS YOU WILL RUE THE DAY YOU ANSWERED HER CALL!!!

OK.

ISN'T THAT JUST LIKE A MAN TO PICK THE ONE THAT REQUIRES THE MOST WORK?

WHY DIDN'T YOU SAY NO WHEN SHE ASKED YOU OUT, IRVING?

I KNOW HOW HARD IT WAS FOR HER TO ASK, CATHY... I KNOW HOW REJECTION HURTS.

YOU'RE THE ONE WHO TAUGHT ME TO BE SUPPORTIVE AND SENSITIVE..... CATHY, HOW COULD I TAMPER WITH THE FRAGILE EGO OF A WOMAN ON THE BRINK OF SELF-REALIZATION?!!

SPLAT.

.. I TRIED.

I WANT TO MAKE UP FOR LAST WEEK, CATHY...LET'S GO SOMEWHERE WARM TOGETHER.

SOMEWHERE WARM?

IMAGINE BASKING ON A HOT BEACH. JUST YOU AND ME.

A HOT BEACH?

HEY, WHAT ARE THE TEARS FOR?

THERE'S ONLY ONE THING THAT CAN MAKE A WOMAN CRY LIKE A ROMANTIC TRIP WITH HER BOYFRIEND, IRVING...

..PUTTING ON A BATHING SUIT IN MARCH!

REALLY? YOU'D RATHER GO ON A SKI TRIP THAN TO SOMEPLACE WARM??

IRVING, I CANNOT PUT ON A BATHING SUIT RIGHT NOW.

THE HUMILIATION OF DISPLAYING THIS BODY ON A BEACH WOULD NOT ONLY NOT BE A VACATION, IT WOULD BE MY WORST NIGHTMARE COME TRUE. TO EVEN THINK ABOUT A BATHING SUIT CAUSES EMBARRASSMENT SO DEEP THAT I CAN BARELY SPEAK.

WELL, YOU SHOULD BRING A SUIT ALONG ANYWAY, CATHY. THEY'LL PROBABLY HAVE A POOL AT THE SKI RESORT.

1986: THE YEAR WE DIDN'T MAKE CONTACT.

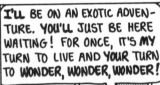

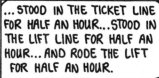

I DO **NOT** IGNORE YOU AS SOON AS A CUTE MAN COMES ALONG, CATHY.

OH, PLEASE, CHARLENE.

YOU'RE LIKE A CHILD WHO NEEDS HER MOTHER TO TAKE HER TO KINDERGARTEN AND THEN WANTS HER TO LEAVE THE SECOND SHE GETS THERE...I CAN'T BELIEVE A GROWN WOMAN IS CAPABLE OF SUCH INFANTILE BEHAVIOR!

BACK SO SOON?

ALL MY CRAYONS BROKE.

I THINK IT'S SO IMPORTANT FOR MEN AND WOMEN TO LEARN TO BE FRIENDS.

YEAH, ME TOO.

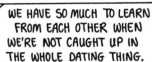

WE HAVE SO MUCH TO LEARN FROM EACH OTHER WHEN WE'RE NOT CAUGHT UP IN THE WHOLE DATING THING.

YEAH.

RELATIONSHIPS COME AND GO, BUT FRIENDSHIP IS FOREVER!!

YEAH...HONEY, COME OVER HERE AND MEET SOME NEW FRIENDS!

NEXT!

THIS IS HEAVEN, CATHY. MEN EVERYWHERE! MEN ON THE LIFTS! MEN IN THE LODGE!

MEN ON VACATION! HAPPY MEN! TALL MEN! SHORT MEN! MUSCLE-Y MEN! RICH MEN! TAN MEN! CUTE MEN!

MEN IN THE RESTAURANTS...MEN IN THE STREETS...MEN IN THE SHOPS...

"MOONLIGHTING" STARTS IN FIVE MINUTES.

...AND OUR FAVORITE: MEN ON TV.

ARE'NT YOU SUSPICIOUS THAT IRVING'S GOING WILD WHILE YOU'RE GONE, CATHY?

NO. I WENT THROUGH ALL MY SUSPICIONS ON MONDAY.

ON TUESDAY I EXPERIENCED JEALOUSY, HOSTILITY, FOUR DIFFERENT INSECURITIES AND TWO FIXATIONS.

TODAY I WRAPPED UP IN A BLANKET OF CONFIDENCE, PUT ON AN AIR OF SUPERIORITY AND DOVE INTO THE DELIRIUM OF PURE FANTASY!!

I CAN'T BELIEVE THIS.

ME EITHER. FOR THE FIRST TIME IN MY LIFE I USED EVERYTHING I BROUGHT WITH ME.

WE'VE SPENT HOURS DISCUSSING WHAT WE'LL SAY WHEN WE SEE OUR BOYFRIENDS.

WE'VE SHOPPED ALL OVER TOWN FOR NEW OUTFITS TO WEAR WHEN WE GREET OUR BOYFRIENDS... WE'VE AGONIZED OVER THE PERFECT GIFTS TO BRING OUR BOYFRIENDS...

...AND WE'VE CALCULATED THE EXACT AMOUNT OF SUN WE NEED FOR TANS THAT WILL DAZZLE OUR BOYFRIENDS.

IT TAKES A FIVE-DAY VACATION TO PREPARE FOR A FIVE-SECOND ENTRANCE.

WHEN IRVING PICKS ME UP AT THE AIRPORT, HE SITS IN HIS CAR OUTSIDE THE BAGGAGE AREA WHILE I LUG 400 POUNDS OF LUGGAGE AROUND TRYING TO FIND HIM.

WHEN ANDREA PICKS ME UP SHE SORT OF WALKS DOWN AND MEETS ME HALFWAY.

WHEN MY MOTHER PICKS ME UP, SHE CAMPS AT THE GATE FOR FOUR HOURS BEFORE THE PLANE LANDS AND SHOWERS ME WITH DEVOTION THE SECOND I GET OFF.

GREETINGS ARE IN INVERSE PROPORTION TO HOW MUCH WE'VE DONE TO DESERVE THEM.

GATE 43

DO YOU EVER LOOK AT THE PAPER AT 8:00, SEE THAT NOTHING GOOD'S GOING TO BE ON TV THAT NIGHT, AND JUST DECIDE TO GO TO BED?

YEAH, I DID THAT ONCE, CATHY. I WAS SO ASHAMED OF MYSELF.

ME TOO... IMAGINE GIVING UP ON THE WHOLE WORLD AT 8:00 AT NIGHT BECAUSE NOTHING'S GOING TO BE ON TV!

DID YOU EVER DO IT AT 8:00 IN THE MORNING?

I WILL **NOT** WEIGH MYSELF THIS MORNING! I FEEL GREAT. THERE'S NO REASON TO WEIGH MYSELF!

I WILL NOT GO NEAR THE SCALE! THE NUMBERS ON THE SCALE ARE MEANINGLESS! I WILL NOT EVEN **THINK** ABOUT WEIGHING MYSELF!

AAACK!!

...IF I WERE THE SORT OF PERSON WHO COULD AVOID TEMPTATION, I WOULDN'T BE IN THIS SITUATION.....

MY CAR IS FROZEN SOLID AND THE TOW TRUCK STILL HASN'T SHOWN UP. I'M GOING TO BE PRETTY LATE, CHARLENE.

WHY DIDN'T YOU JUST ASK IRVING TO GIVE YOU A RIDE TODAY, CATHY?

IRVING'S A LITTLE ANNOYED WITH ME THIS WEEK.

YOU COULDN'T HAVE GOTTEN ALONG FOR ONE LITTLE RIDE??

IT'S A QUESTION OF PRINCIPLE, CHARLENE...

...I'D RATHER SPEND THE MORNING WITH A FROZEN ENGINE THAN FIVE SECONDS WITH A COLD SHOULDER.

THE BABY WILL BE HERE IN TWO MONTHS! HI, BABY! THIS IS DADDY!

DADDY. AACK! I'M NOT READY FOR DADDY.. AACK. NO. I'M FINE. FINE. I'VE READ THE BOOK. I'VE SEEN THE MOVIE. I'VE RENTED THE VIDEO. HA, HA. NO. FEAR IS NORMAL. HA. NO. I'M **FINE**. EVERYTHING IS..

..AAACK WHO ARE YOU AND WHAT IS A PREGNANT WOMAN DOING IN MY LIVING ROOM??!!

AT SEVEN MONTHS THEY START BABBLING.

SO...UH..HOW LONG DOES THE TAPE OF YOUR UNBORN BABY'S HEARTBEAT **LAST**??

OH, IT'S LOOPED SO WE CAN LISTEN TO IT ALL EVENING!!

THUMPA THUMPA THUMPA THUMPA THUMPA THUMPA THUMPA THUMPA

HERE'S A PICTURE OF THE ULTRASOUND FETAL IMAGE!

IT WAS WAVING! HI, HONEY! IT'S MOMMY!!

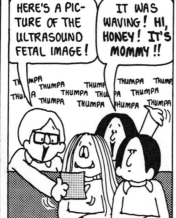

THUMPA THUMPA THUMPA THUMPA THUMPA THUMPA

HERE'S A VIDEOTAPE OF ANDREA'S BARE STOMACH MOVING WHEN THE BABY KICKS!

AND HERE'S A PHOTO ESSAY ON THE ACTUAL BIRTH PROCESS!

THUMPA THUMPA THUMPA THUMPA THUMPA THUMPA

...OH, BUT DON'T WORRY, CATHY. HAVING THIS BABY ISN'T GOING TO MAKE US ANY DIFFERENT WITH OUR FRIENDS!

THAT'S WHAT WE'RE AFRAID OF.

THUMPA THUMPA THUMPA THUMPA THUMPA THUMPA THUMPA THUMPA THUMPA

BONNE NUIT, MON BÉBÉ!

NOW YOU'RE SPEAKING FRENCH TO YOUR UNBORN CHILD THROUGH A PAPER TOWEL TUBE??

IT'S PROVEN THAT A BABY CAN LEARN TO RECOGNIZE VOICES AND SIMPLE WORDS BEFORE BIRTH, CATHY...

...SO WHY NOT INTRODUCE THE CONCEPT OF FOREIGN LANGUAGE?

BUONA NOTTE, BAMBINO.

IT KICKED!!

TRILINGUAL!!

SHEESH.

OY VAY.

IN ORDER TO SEND MESSAGES EFFICIENTLY, A PERSON'S NERVE CELLS MUST BE COATED WITH A SHEATH OF PROTEIN CALLED "MYELIN".

WITH SENSORY STIMULATION EXERCISES, I CAN NOT ONLY SPEED THE MYELINATION PROCESS IN MY UNBORN BABY, HAVING A DIRECT EFFECT ON COORDINATION AND INTELLECT...

...BUT I CAN ACTUALLY ENCOURAGE THE ELONGATION OF AXONS AND BRANCHING OF DENDRITES THAT ARE SO ESSENTIAL FOR THE GROWTH OF MY BABY'S BRAIN AND DEVELOPMENT OF ITS ENTIRE BODY!

ALL I EVER DID WAS KNIT YOU BOOTIES!!

HAVE YOU PAINTED THE BABY'S ROOM YET, ANDREA?

NO, BUT WE **HAVE** BOUGHT BABY'S FIRST ISOKINETIC WORKOUT WAGON... AN ERGONOMIC STROLLER...COMPACT DISC MUSICAL MOBILE... A PC WITH INTERACTIVE, PRE-VERBAL SOFTWARE...A "BUSY BOX" WITH 32-DIGIT AUTO-REDIAL...

CRIB SHEETS PRINTED WITH THE WORKS OF THE 17TH-CENTURY MASTERS.... FLASH CARDS... ENOUGH LEGO SETS TO RECONSTRUCT MANHATTAN...NONTOXIC MARKERS COLOR COORDINATED WITH BABY'S HANDLOOMED VCR COVER... AND A STUFFED LEMUR THAT PLAYS THE OPERAS OF PUCCINI!!

HAVE YOU PAINTED THE BABY'S CONDOMINIUM YET?

EVERY BITE OF FOOD I EAT AFFECTS MY BABY. THE RESPONSIBILITY IS STAGGERING.

EVERY MORSEL OF FOOD I CHOOSE FOR MYSELF WILL ACTUALLY IMPACT THE LIFE OF ANOTHER HUMAN BEING!

WELL, IF YOU'RE GOING TO BLOW YOUR DIET WITH PIE, MOM, I GUESS I CAN TOO.

BAD NEWS, ANDREA. IT DOESN'T STOP WITH BIRTH.

LOOK AT THE EXCELLENT SALE ON VALENTINE CANDY, CATHY!

MY! WHAT A FINE VALUE, MOM!

½ off VALENTINE CANDY SALE

CANDY FREEZES SO NICELY. MAYBE I'LL GET A SMALL BOX FOR THE FREEZER.

YES! WHY NOT PICK UP AN EXTRA?

½ off VALENTINE CANDY SALE

IT'S ALWAYS GOOD TO HAVE CHOCOLATE IN THE FREEZER FOR COMPANY!

YES! FOR THE COMPANY!

STOCK UP WHILE THE PRICE IS LOW!

HOW FRUGAL! HOW THRIFTY!

WHO ARE WE KIDDING?

WHO CARES?

Guisewite

PRINCE ANDREW IS GETTING MARRIED, CATHY.

NO PROBLEM. I'M NOT HAVING A CRISIS OVER THIS ONE, CHARLENE.

HE GAVE HIS FIANCÉE AN ENGAGEMENT RING WORTH $35,000.

NO PROBLEM. NO REGRETS. I'M COOL.

HE WAS TOO YOUNG FOR US.

WAAAH!!

HERE WE GO AGAIN.

THE 5-YEAR CD HAS AN EXCELLENT YIELD FOR YOUR IRA.

5 YEARS?! OH, NO. TOO LONG. NO. 5 YEARS? AACK. NO.

IRA COUNSELER

THE 2-YEAR CD IS ALSO QUITE GOOD.

2 YEARS?! NO. WHAT IF SOMETHING BETTER COMES ALONG? NO WAY. NO. 2 YEARS? NO.

THE 90-DAY ACCOUNT IS ALSO A POSSIBILITY.

90 DAYS. I'M NOT READY. I'M NOT SURE. OK. YES. AACK! NO. WAIT. I NEED MORE TIME. NO. OK. 90 DAYS. I'LL TRY FOR 90 DAYS.

FINE. NOW, ARE YOU SINGLE?

HOW'D YOU GUESS?

IRA COUNSELER

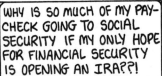

WHY IS SO MUCH OF MY PAYCHECK GOING TO SOCIAL SECURITY IF MY ONLY HOPE FOR FINANCIAL SECURITY IS OPENING AN IRA??!

IRA QUESTIONS

WHY DO I GET THE FEELING THAT THE $2,000 I PUT IN AN IRA TODAY WILL BE WORTH 10¢ BY THE TIME I CAN GET IT OUT??

WHY ISN'T THE CUTE MAN FROM YOUR TV COMMERCIAL HERE NOW WHEN WE NEED HIM??!

IRA

WHY DID I CHOOSE A CAREER IN BANKING?

IRA QUESTIONS

100

CATHY'S BEEN IN THERE DOING HER TAXES FOR HOURS!

IT ISN'T JUST DOING TAXES.

THIS IS THE ONE TIME OF THE YEAR WHEN WE'RE FORCED TO REALLY FACE FACTS AND FIND NEW WAYS TO COPE.

ACROSS THE NATION, PEOPLE ARE HUNCHED OVER DESKS TONIGHT, MAKING DISCOVER-IES THAT WILL CHANGE THEIR WHOLE LIVES...

I CAN EAT 4 "THIN MINTS" FOR ONLY 25 MORE CALORIES THAN IN 2 "DO-SI-DOS"!!

WHY DID I WAIT UNTIL THE LAST SECOND TO DO MY TAXES? ...BECAUSE I GREW UP WATCH-ING YOU WAIT UNTIL THE LAST SECOND TO DO YOUR TAXES!

WHY ARE A YEAR'S RECEIPTS WADDED UP IN MY JUNK DRAWER?...BECAUSE YOU KEPT RECEIPTS WADDED UP IN YOUR JUNK DRAWER!

I WORSHIPPED YOU! I MODELED MY WHOLE LIFE AFTER YOU AND NOW I HAVE BECOME YOU!! YOUR VERY OWN JUNIOR SCRAP PAPER FACTORY!!!

DO WE WEEP FOR JOY OR JUST WEEP?

HOW COULD TAXES BE DUE NEXT WEEK, IRVING?? HOW?!

CATHY, WHY DOES TAX TIME ALWAYS SHOCK YOU?!

APRIL 15 COMES EVERY YEAR! THERE ARE ADS, SIGNS, AR-TICLES...WHOLE BUSINESSES DEVOTED TO APRIL 15!

HOW COULD YOU BE ALIVE AND NOT KNOW THAT YOU'RE SUP-POSED TO DO SOMETHING ABOUT APRIL 15?!!

I RELATE TO TAX TIME THE WAY YOU RELATE TO VALENTINE'S DAY.

NO MONEY. NO SAVINGS.

NO INVESTMENTS. NO PROGRESS. NO HOPE.

WE ALL GET DEMORALIZED, CATHY. YOU JUST HAVE TO LEARN TO PICK YOURSELF UP BY YOUR OWN BOOTSTRAPS!

NO STRAPS.

I'D LOVE TO SEE YOU TONIGHT, CATHY, BUT IT'S A PRETTY BUSY DAY.

"BUSY": HE'LL BE AT THE OFFICE UNTIL MIDNIGHT.

I TOLD TOM I'D GRAB A BITE WITH HIM TOMORROW.

"GRAB A BITE": THEY'LL PLAY RACQUETBALL UNTIL 10:00 P.M.

YOU'RE SO UNDERSTANDING.

"SO UNDERSTANDING": HE'LL CALL SUNDAY NIGHT, AFTER IT'S TOO LATE TO GO OUT.

WHY DO YOU KEEP DATING HIM, CATHY??

I HATE TO LEAVE THE COUNTRY NOW THAT I'VE FINALLY LEARNED THE LANGUAGE.

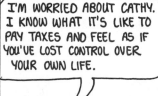

I'M WORRIED ABOUT CATHY. I KNOW WHAT IT'S LIKE TO PAY TAXES AND FEEL AS IF YOU'VE LOST CONTROL OVER YOUR OWN LIFE.

THE GOVERNMENT TAKES AND SPENDS ALL YOUR MONEY AT NO TIME DO HARD-WORKING PEOPLE FEEL SO UTTERLY AND COMPLETELY HELPLESS.

DING DONG

I BELIEVE CATHY'S SENSE OF POWER HAS BEEN RESTORED, DEAR.

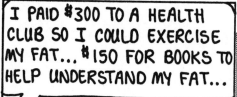   

 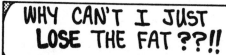  

CHARLENE!
MR. PINKLEY WANTS YOU.
HE'S FAKING IT. HE JUST WANTS ATTENTION.

Cha·a·rleene!!
OVER-DRAMATICS. HE'S TESTING ME.

CHARLENE.
THIS TIME HE MIGHT REALLY NEED SOMETHING.

LIKE A MOTHER BABOON, WE INSTINCTIVELY INTERPRET THE CRIES OF OUR YOUNG.

"TO CHARLENE FOR SECRE-TARIES WEEK: SURE, WE'RE MOVING IN THE COMPUTERS... THE COLLATORS... THE PRINTERS... THE DIALERS...

THE POSTAGE MACHINES... THE ADDING MACHINES... THE COPY MACHINES... THE COFFEE MACHINES... THE TELEX MACHINES...

...BUT IT'S STILL THE **PEOPLE** WHO MAKE THE DIFFERENCE."

FUSE BOX
PRODUCT TESTING, INC
CLICK!
OFF
OFF
OFF
ON OFF

FOR YOUNGER, HEALTHIER HAIR... FOR YOUNGER, FIRMER SKIN....

FOR YOUNGER EYES... FOR YOUNGER HANDS... FOR YOUNGER LIPS... LOOK YOUNGER...FEEL YOUNG-ER.. BE YOUNGER..YOUNG! YOUNG. YOUNG..

SPLASH SQUIRT DAB SQUIRT FLUFF PUFF

READY FOR WORK, CATHY?

AFTER 20 YEARS OF CHEERING WOMEN ON TO BE ALL THEY CAN BE, A STUDY WAS PUBLISHED LAST MONTH BRANDING THOSE SAME TRIUMPHANT WOMEN AS "OLD MAIDS" IF NOT MARRIED BY THEIR EARLY 30s.

NEWS

WHILE THE "SPINSTER SURVEY" WAS TOO ABSURD TO BE TAKEN SERIOUSLY BY ANYONE...

NEWS

...SOME PARTICULARLY ASTUTE WOMEN HAVE BEEN ABLE TO UTILIZE ITS FINDINGS AS A SPRINGBOARD FOR MEANINGFUL DIALOGUES WITH THEIR MALE COUNTERPARTS.

NEWS

WHAT'S IT TO YOU, YOU OLD GEEZER?!!

SNICKER SNICKER

"...A SINGLE 25-YEAR-OLD WOMAN HAS ONLY A 50% CHANCE OF MARRYING... A 30-YEAR-OLD HAS ONLY A 20% CHANCE... A 35-YEAR-OLD HAS.."...WELL, THAT'S LUDICROUS.

YEAH...I GUESS IT IS, MOM.

LOOK AT YOU, CATHY! BY NOT JUMPING INTO MARRIAGE, YOU'VE BECOME SUCCESSFUL, CONFIDENT, DYNAMIC, BEAUTIFUL....

..WHY, YOU'RE ONE IN A MILLION!!

WAAHH!!

I NEVER KNOW WHEN TO QUIT.

ONLY A WOMAN FRIEND COULD UNDERSTAND HOW IT FEELS TO READ A SURVEY THAT IMPLIES A WOMAN IS A TOTAL REJECT IF SHE ISN'T MARRIED.

OOF.

MY MOTHER JUST GETS THAT "I TOLD YOU SO" LOOK. MY MEN FRIENDS GET THE "I TOLD YOU SO" LOOK.

OOF!

ONLY YOU HAVE THAT PAINED LOOK THAT TELLS ME WE SHARE THE SAME INNER TURMOIL.

OOF! THE BABY'S KICKING!

...BACK TO YOU, FLUFFY.

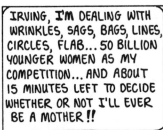

HIT ME IN THE STOMACH, CATHY! SOLID AS A ROCK! GO AHEAD!

PUNCH ME IN THE ARM! LIKE IRON. I FEEL NOTHING.

CRUSH MY FISTS... STOMP ON MY HEART... ATTACK MY EGO... I AM INVINCIBLE !!

OH, IRVING, YOU DON'T HAVE TO PROVE...

«PAT PAT

AACK! DON'T TOUCH MY HAIR! IT MIGHT FALL OUT!

Guisewite

"MINOXIDIL" IS USED TO TREAT HIGH BLOOD PRESSURE AND YOU'RE PUTTING IT ON YOUR HEAD, IRVING?

YOU'RE TRYING TO GROW HAIR USING HIGH BLOOD PRESSURE MEDICINE??

SOME PEOPLE THINK IT WORKS.

ARE MEN CRAZY? HAVE YOU TOTALLY LOST TRACK OF WHAT MAKES SENSE??!

...OH, WILL YOU BRING ME SOME ANTACID? I DIDN'T GET MY R.D.A. OF CALCIUM YET TODAY.

Guisewite

WHEN A DAUGHTER BECOMES AWARE OF HER OWN AGING, IT CHANGES HER PERSPECTIVE ON EVERYONE.

LINE SAL

SUDDENLY THE WOMAN SHE'S SPENT HER LIFE EITHER IGNORING OR RIDICULING BECOMES THE VERY WOMAN SHE RUNS TO FOR ADVICE.

IT'S THE DAY A MOTHER WAITS FOR ALL HER LIFE...

HELP ME !!

COSMETIC

WRINKLE CREMES

...AND IT'S CALLED "TOMORROW."

COSMETICS

WRINKLE CREME

Guisewite

EVERY YEAR I TORTURE MY-SELF ABOUT ALL THE THINGS I BUY TRYING TO GET BEAUTIFUL FOR SUMMER.

DRESSES TO MAKE ME LOOK THIN...MAKEUP TO MAKE ME LOOK TAN...SUNGLASSES TO MAKE ME LOOK COOL... WHY...WHY...WHY...

FOR ONCE IN MY LIFE I'M JUST GOING TO RELAX THIS YEAR AND ACCEPT MYSELF AS I AM.

VAIN.

THAT WILL BE $72.50.

summer fashions

Guisewite

FOR YEARS I COULD BUY NOTHING BECAUSE GAS WAS SO EXPENSIVE.

NOW SELF-SERVE GAS IS SO CHEAP I'VE ACTUALLY SAVED UP SOME MONEY.

IN FACT, LIKE MILLIONS OF AMERICANS, I'VE SAVED SO MUCH BY CONSISTENTLY USING SELF-SERVE GAS THAT I CAN NOW AFFORD SOMETHING I NEVER DREAMED OF OWNING...

..A NEW ENGINE TO REPLACE THE ONE THAT BLEW BECAUSE I NEVER GET MY OIL CHECKED ANYMORE.

Guisewite

YOU'RE PAYING $90 TO GET A TAN IN-SIDE A BUILDING, CATHY??

YES.

YOU'RE GOING TO LOCK YOURSELF IN A LITTLE ROOM, UNDRESS, AND LIE ON A BED OF LIGHT BULBS WHILE A 900-POUND LID CLOSES OVER YOU, TURNING YOU INTO A HUMAN HOT DOG??!

YES.

WHY DON'T YOU JUST GO OUTSIDE IN A BATHING SUIT?

AACK NOT THAT!!

WE ALL HAVE OUR LIMITS.

Guisewite

112

YOU DIET THE SAME WAY YOU ARGUE, CATHY. YOU NEVER FINISH.

YOU KEEP GOING BACK AND FORTH OVER THE EXACT SAME THING WITHOUT EVER RE-SOLVING ANYTHING.

FOR ONCE WHY CAN'T YOU JUST STICK TO THE DIET, FINISH THE ARGUMENT AND MOVE ON TO SOMETHING NEW?

THE BURDEN ALWAYS FALLS ON THE WOMAN TO MAKE THINGS LAST.

Panel 1:
I'M A LITTLE NERVOUS ABOUT STARTING MY INDOOR TANNING, ANDREA.

YOU NEED MORE FACTS, CATHY.

Panel 2:
WHO MANUFACTURES THE TANNING BEDS? WHAT'S THE PERCENTAGE OF UV-B TO UV-A RAYS? WHAT'S THE SCIENTIFIC COMMUNITY'S RESPONSE TO CLAIMS OF "SAFE, NON-PREMATURE-AGING TANNING"?

Panel 3:
GET ON THE PHONE AND GET THE ANSWERS YOU NEED TO FEEL SAFE!!

Panel 4:
WOULD ANYONE I KNOW EVER SEE ME GOING IN THERE?

Panel 5:
WHAT IF THEY SET THE TIMER WRONG? WHAT IF THE LID IS STUCK? I THINK MY SKIN IS MELTING. I'M ALLERGIC TO LIGHT BULBS. THEY FORGOT I'M IN HERE. AACK! WHERE'S THE ESCAPE BUTTON?!!

Panel 6:
AAACK!! EVERYONE WENT HOME AND LEFT ME TO FRY LIKE A LITTLE BEETLE BUT I ESCAPED! I'M FREE!! I LIVED! I...

Panel 7:
OOPS.

Panel 8:
SOME PEOPLE GET MORE COLOR FROM THE FIRST TANNING SESSION THAN OTHERS.

TANNING INFO.

Panel 9:
THEY SAY THE PERCENTAGE OF MEN WHO ARE LOSING THEIR HAIR IS THE SAME AS A MAN'S AGE, CATHY.

Panel 10:
AT AGE 40, 40% OF THE MEN ARE LOSING THEIR HAIR... AT AGE 60, 60% OF THE MEN ARE LOSING THEIR HAIR...

Panel 11:
AT AGE 30...

IN THE LAST 20 SECONDS, YOU'VE EATEN ENOUGH CALORIES TO SUSTAIN A 115-POUND WOMAN FOR TWO DAYS, IRVING.

Panel 12:
YOU WOMEN HAVE SUCH ONE-TRACK MINDS.

CATHY, THE TANNING BOOTH IS FINE FOR A START...BUT YOU CAN'T JUST SIT IN THERE ALL BY YOURSELF ALL SUMMER.

WHY NOT? I LIKE IT IN HERE.

BOOTH #5

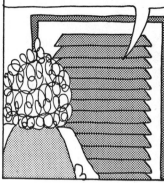

I'M GETTING TAN FOR THE FIRST TIME IN MY LIFE AND NO ONE HAS TO SEE MY FLAB.

AREN'T YOU FORGETTING WHAT'S REALLY IMPORTANT....WHAT GIVES OUR LIVES PURPOSE AND MEANING?

YEAH, I GUESS YOU'RE RIGHT.

HAND IN A DIET SODA.

BOOTH #5

YOU HAVEN'T EVEN PLANNED ANDREA'S SHOWER YET??

NAH... THERE'S PLENTY OF TIME.

HER BABY'S DUE IN THREE WEEKS, CATHY! IT'S NORMAL FOR WOMEN WHO ARE CONFUSED ABOUT MOTHERHOOD TO EXPRESS SOME DENIAL, BUT...

DENIAL?? DON'T BE RIDICULOUS, MOM! I'M THRILLED ABOUT ANDREA'S BABY!!

WHAT BABY?

WHEN YOU'RE PREGNANT, TOTAL STRANGERS THINK THEY CAN WALK UP AND PAT YOU ON THE STOMACH, CATHY.

NO MATTER WHAT ELSE YOU'VE ACCOMPLISHED, ALL PEOPLE WANT TO HEAR ABOUT IS YOUR PREGNANCY! WHEN ARE YOU DUE... IS THIS YOUR FIRST....

HI, ANDREA. HOW'S THE CAREER GOING?

WHAT'S THE MATTER, YOU DON'T LIKE BABIES?!!

CARRYING THIS BABY MAKES ME WONDER IF I WAS TOO CRITICAL OF YOUR RELATIONSHIPS, CATHY.

RELAX, CATHY. TAKE A DEEP, CLEANSING BREATH!

CLICK

GASP PANT

YOU PROBABLY WOULD HAVE YOUR OWN LITTLE FAMILY BY NOW IF IT WEREN'T FOR ME!

TRANSITIONAL BREATHING! OUT, OUT, IN! OUT, OUT, IN!

"PANT PANT!"   "PANT PANT!"

I JUST HOPE YOU CAN PICK UP THE SHREDS OF YOUR LIFE AND FIND THIS KIND OF FULFILLMENT.

PUSH, CATHY, PUSH OUT THAT DOOR!

ANOTHER PERFECT DELIVERY MADE POSSIBLE BY LAMAZE.

THROW OUT LAST MONTH'S MAGAZINES...THROW OUT LAST WEEK'S NEWSPAPERS...THROW OUT LAST YEAR'S REVIEWS...

THROW OUT THE ARTICLES I'LL NEVER GET TO...THE STUDIES I'LL NEVER STUDY...THE PROGRAMS I'LL NEVER LOOK AT.....EXPIRED INSURANCE OFFERS...EXTINCT INVESTMENTS...NEWSLETTERS...MEMOS...PAMPHLETS...NOTES...IDEAS...CONTESTS...CAUSES...ADVICE....

CATHY, DID YOU SEE THE TELEVISION SHOW ON...

TELEVISION?? I HAVE NO TIME FOR TELEVISION!

IT TAKES ME FULL TIME TO THROW AWAY MY READING MATERIAL.

IS YOUR TV SET TURNED OFF?

YES, THE TV IS OFF, ANDREA. IT'S SAFE TO BRING YOUR UNBORN BABY INTO THE ROOM.

SORRY, CATHY...BUT EXCEPT FOR THE ONE TIME I ACCIDENTALLY WALKED PAST A TV PLAYING SATURDAY MORNING CARTOONS, MY BABY HAS ONLY BEEN EXPOSED TO PBS.

FOR 8½ MONTHS LUKE AND I HAVE SAT TOGETHER AND LISTENED TO HOURS OF FASCINATING EDUCATIONAL PROGRAMS WITH OUR FETUS.

WE CAN'T WAIT TO FIND OUT WHAT ITS WONDROUS NEW MIND HAS RETAINED!

HORDAK! SKELETOR! HE-MAN! FROSTED FLAKES!

WHAT DO I FILL OUT TO BEGIN MY MATERNITY LEAVE?

WE HAVE NO MATERNITY LEAVE HERE.

PERSONNEL

WHAT??

OH, NO. LIKE MANY AMERICAN COMPANIES, WE TREAT GIVING BIRTH TO A HUMAN BEING JUST AS WE WOULD IF YOU SKIPPED TOWN FOR A BOWLING CONVENTION.

NO LEAVE. NO PAY. NO JOB WHEN YOU COME BACK.

I THINK I'M GOING TO BE SICK.

BETTER SAVE IT. YOU ONLY HAVE 3 DAYS OF PAID SICK TIME COMING.

PERSONNEL

NO MATERNITY LEAVE?? YOU MEAN I HAVE TO QUIT MY JOB TO SPEND TIME WITH MY NEWBORN??

PERSONNEL

DON'T BE SILLY. THIS IS 1986.

YOU CAN QUIT... YOU CAN BE FIRED... YOU CAN GO BROKE HIRING BABY SITTERS... OR, YOU CAN COLLAPSE FROM EXHAUSTION TRYING TO DO IT ALL!

WHAT DID YOU FIND OUT?

WE HAVE OPTIONS OUR MOTHERS NEVER DREAMED OF.

OF 117 DEMOCRATIC NATIONS IN THE WORLD, THE UNITED STATES IS THE ONLY ONE WITH NO GUARANTEED MATERNITY LEAVE.

INCREDIBLE!

BABY CONGRATULATIONS

A NEW MOTHER'S "OPTIONS" ARE: GET FIRED, GO BROKE, OR COLLAPSE FROM EXHAUSTION.

EVEN THE SOVIET UNION GIVES A 6-MONTH LEAVE WITH FULL PAY!

UNTIL BUSINESSES QUIT TREATING PARENTING AS A HOBBY, WE'RE DOOMING OURSELVES TO A NATION OF FRUSTRATED, GUILTY ADULTS AND RAISING WHOLE GENERATIONS OF BABIES WHO NEVER EVEN HAD THE BONDING OF A 24-HOUR PARENT IN THE FIRST PRECIOUS WEEKS OF LIFE!!

HOW I LOVE THE GIGGLING AND GABBING OF A BABY SHOWER!

Come in

WHO WILL HAVE COFFEE?

IS IT DECAFFEINATED? CHEMICALLY DECAFFEINATED OR WATER-PROCESS DECAFFEINATED? FRESH GROUND BEANS? MADE WITH PURE SPRING WATER? STORED IN GLASS? AT ROOM TEMPERATURE? BREWED BY THE CHEMEX METHOD?

WHO WILL HAVE PIE?

......WAS IT NATURAL?...

TA DA! ONE YEAR LATER, ANDREA, AND I FINALLY GOT A WHOLE BAG OF MICROWAVE POPCORN TO POP!

A YEAR... HM....

DO YOU REALIZE THAT A YEAR AGO I HADN'T EVEN MET LUKE YET, CATHY??

IN ONE YEAR I MET A PERFECT MAN...HAD A PERFECT WEDDING...RESTRUCTURED MY WHOLE LIFE... AND CREATED AN ENTIRE, NEW HUMAN BEING!!

SO MANY WOMEN LET THEIR BABIES TAKE OVER THEIR WHOLE LIVES, CATHY.

WE'RE NOT GOING TO DO THAT WHEN YOU'RE BORN, ARE WE, LITTLE ONE?...NO! NO-EY, WO-EY!

BABY HAS TO LEARN THAT MOMMY HAS...OOH! BABY MOVED! DOES BABY WANT MOMMY TO MOVE? SHOULD MOMMY READ A STORY? IS BABY TIRED? SHOULD MOMMY SING? HI, BABY! MOMMY LOVES BABY! HI, BABY!

HOW REFRESHING TO SEE A MOTHER WITH A FIRM GRIP ON HER OWN IDENTITY.

Panel 1: WHERE'S THE LIST OF NAMES YOU'VE PICKED OUT FOR YOUR BABY, CATHY? | LIST?? WHY DO YOU HAVE A LIST?!

Panel 2: ME?? A LIST?? OH, HA, HA! THAT CHARLENE, WHAT A KIDDER!

Panel 3: I CHERISH MY SINGLE LIFE! I LOVE MY FREE-DOM! WHEW! LIST! HOO-BOY, NO! I'M NOT READY FOR ANY LIST!!

Panel 4: WHERE'S THE LIST, CATHY? | RIGHT HERE UNDER THE LIST OF SONGS I'VE PICKED OUT FOR MY WEDDING.

Panel 5: TO HELP CREATE THE MOTHER-CHILD BOND, I PLAY THIS TAPE OF MY VOICE THROUGH LITTLE HEADPHONES PLACED AGAINST THE TUMMY.

Panel 6: ANDREA, MY MOTHER NEVER DID THAT AND LOOK AT US. I DEPEND ON HER APPROVAL.... I BEG FOR HER ADVICE... I RUN TO HER FOR COMFORT...

Panel 7: I'M A GROWN WOMAN AND I CAN'T GET THROUGH A WEEK WITHOUT CALLING HER 75 TIMES!!

Panel 8: WE'RE NOT BONDED... WE'RE CRAZY-GLUED! | CLICK!

Panel 9: ...A BLUE AND PINK RATTLE. NO. ALL WRONG. THE RODS AND CONES OF A NEWBORN'S EYES HAVE NOT MATURED ENOUGH TO PERCEIVE COLOR VALUES.

Panel 10: ...A STATIONARY SEAT. NO GOOD. NO WAY. A BABY NEEDS LINEAR ROCKING TO STIMU-LATE NEUROMUSCULAR COOR-DINATION AND WEIGHT GAIN.

Panel 11: ...SILENT DUCK MOBILE. WRONG, WRONG, WRONG! DON'T PEOPLE KNOW TOYS HAVE TO STIMULATE BOTH THE RIGHT AND LEFT SIDES OF THE BRAIN TO PROMOTE INTELLIGENCE?!!

Panel 12: WHAT GIFTS DO YOU WANT FOR YOUR BABY, ANDREA? | OH, ANY-THING WOULD BE WONDERFUL!

OH, CHARLENE, LOOK! ISN'T THIS CUTE??

I LOVE THIS ONE, CATHY!

CHILDREN'S DEPART

THIS IS THE ONE I'LL GET!...NO, THIS ONE!

NO...THIS ONE! I HAVE TO GET THIS ONE!

THERE'S NO SUCH THING AS TOO MANY STUFFED TOYS!

STUFFED TOYS HELP DEVELOP THE IMAGINATION!

AW...HOW OLD IS THE BABY?

WHAT BABY?

CHILDREN'S CHECK-OUT

DO YOU WANT A BOY OR A GIRL?

OH, FOR HEAVEN'S SAKE, CHARLENE.

ANDREA'S NINE MONTHS PREGNANT! THERE'S ONLY ONE QUESTION THAT MATTERS!

THANK YOU, CATHY.

HOW MUCH WEIGHT HAVE YOU GAINED?

HI, BABY. THIS IS MOMMY.

AND THIS IS DADDY. WE CAN'T WAIT TO MEET YOU!

WE WANT TO SEE YOUR SWEET FACE...WE WANT TO TOUCH YOUR LITTLE TOES...BUT YOU KNOW WHY WE WANT YOU BORN MOST OF ALL?...

MOMMY FEELS LIKE A WALRUS.

AT 3:00 AM I WAS STANDING IN THE 7-ELEVEN SCREAMING BECAUSE I COULDN'T WRITE A CHECK FOR A PEANUT BUTTER CUP.... FROM THAT MOMENT ON, I KNEW I'D NEVER CHEAT ON MY DIET!

I SNEAKED INTO MY BOYFRIEND'S KITCHEN, MADE CINNAMON ROLLS OUT OF STALE HAMBURGER BUNS AND ATE THEM ALL WHILE HE WAS ASLEEP...FROM THAT MOMENT ON, I KNEW I'D NEVER CHEAT ON MY DIET!

I CHIPPED A CANDY BAR OUT OF THE MAP POCKET OF MY CAR WHERE IT MELTED TWO SUMMERS AGO.... FROM THAT MOMENT ON, I KNEW I'D NEVER CHEAT ON MY DIET!

WE DON'T BELONG IN THIS GROUP, CATHY.

I KNOW. NONE OF THAT WOULD HAVE EVEN SLOWED ME DOWN.

Guisewite

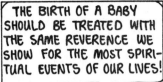

ARE YOU GOING TO THE BIRTH OF ANDREA'S BABY, CATHY?

GOING?? ARE YOU CRAZY, MR. PINKLEY?

THE BIRTH OF A BABY SHOULD BE TREATED WITH THE SAME REVERENCE WE SHOW FOR THE MOST SPIRITUAL EVENTS OF OUR LIVES!

ANDREA'S DILATED TO FIVE CENTIMETERS!

I'LL JUST WATCH IT ON TV.

THE '80s WOMAN ARRIVES AT THE MATERNITY WARD LIKE A ONE-WOMAN BIRTHING BRIGADE.

SHE'S STUDIED DOZENS OF BOOKS, GONE TO CLASSES, ATTENDED SEMINARS, SEEN FILMS, MEMORIZED CHARTS, AND TRAINED LIKE AN OLYMPIC ATHLETE FOR 9 MONTHS.

ACUTELY AWARE OF WHAT EVERY SINGLE CELL IN HER BODY IS DOING, SHE TENSES WITH ANIMAL INSTINCT FOR THE BIGGEST CHALLENGE OF HER LIFE....

ADMISSIONS DESK

...TRYING TO CONVINCE SOMEONE SHE'S HAVING A BABY.

NAH..GO ON HOME. YOU DON'T LOOK READY YET.

FUNNY, ISN'T IT, THAT IT'S US -THE WOODSTOCK GENERATION- WHO ARE LEADING THE WAY IN DRUG-FREE CHILDBIRTH?

ALL THAT TIME OF TAKING DRUGS FOR NO REASON.... AND NOW WE WOULDN'T EVEN THINK OF TAKING AN ASPIRIN!

NOW, WHEN I'M TRYING TO PUSH A SEVEN-POUND HUMAN BEING OUT OF MY BODY, ALL I NEED IS HERBAL TEA, CALMING MUSIC AND...

...ETHER! I WANT ETHER!!

EVERYTHING OK?

YEAH, JUST A LITTLE NOSTALGIA.